SUNRISE to STARLIGHT

SUNRISE to STARLIGHT

an anthology of man's day in prose and poetry

compiled by

MAY DETHERAGE

nashville * abingdon press * new york

SUNRISE TO STARLIGHT

Copyright © 1966 by Abingdon Press

All rights reserved.

Library of Congress Catalog Number: 66-21969

SET UP, PRINTED, AND BOUND BY THE
PARTHENON PRESS, AT NASHVILLE,
TENNESSEE, UNITED STATES OF AMERICA

"A Day," by William L. Stidger, is used by permission
of Mrs. Elizabeth S. Hyland. "God Give Me Joy" is
reprinted through the permission of First Church of
Christ, Scientist, of Maywood, Illinois, from *1000
Quotable Poems,* by Thomas Curtis Clark. "Of Ancient
Shackles" is used by permission of Adelaide Love.
"When There Is Music" by David Morton, from
Journey into Time, copyright 1958 by The Pentelic
Press; used by permission. "Lover to Lover" by David
Morton is used by permission of Mrs. Martha Rutan.
"Death Is a Door" by Nancy Byrd Turner is reprinted
by permission of Dodd, Mead & Company from *Star
in a Well* by Nancy Byrd Turner; copyright 1935 by
Dodd, Mead & Company, Inc. "Work" by Angela
Morgan is reprinted by permission of Dodd, Mead &
Company from *The Hour Has Struck* by Angela
Morgan; copyright 1914 by Angela Morgan. "This,
Too, Will Pass" from *Songs of Hope* by Grace Noll
Crowell; copyright 1938 by Harper & Brothers; "The
Common Tasks" from *Light of the Years* by Grace
Noll Crowell; copyright 1937, 1939, 1941 by Harper &
Brothers; both reprinted by permission of Harper &
Row, Publishers. Selections from *The Choice to Love*
by Robert Raynolds are used by permission of Harper
& Row, Publishers. Selections from *Gift from the
Sea,* by Anne Morrow Lindbergh; © copyright 1955
by Anne Morrow Lindbergh; reprinted by permission
of Pantheon Books, A Division of Random House,
Inc. "Refuge" from *The Collected Poems of Lew
Sarett;* copyright, 1941, by Henry Holt and Company;
copyright transferred, 1955, to Alma Johnson Sarett;
reprinted by permission of Mrs. Sarett. Selections

The compiler is indebted to Miss Nelle C. Davidson, Librarian, and Dr. Helen E. Falls, Professor, of the New Orleans Baptist Theological Seminary, for their generous help in research for this anthology.

dedicated to
MY MOTHER
who showed me love

PREFACE

This compilation of prose, poetry, and terse sayings is done for the pleasure of the reader.

For a framework in which to list the items recorded here the idea of a day—or a man's lifetime—is used.

Dawn is that early, first brush with life when all the world belongs "to me" and every new discovery is a thrill. Morning is a youth time when action, dreams, and adventures are putting into shape character. Noontime is the heat of struggle with life in vocation, in society, and in all areas of living. It is when the controls are in hand and decisions are hard and fast. It is the "go" time. Evening is a time of arrival, of being, of authority. Evening gathers up what Dawn saw, Morning investigated, Noon accomplished, and in the reaping is storing up or sharing the returns. Nighttime is the threshold of rest.

It is the desire of the compiler that in whatever hour the reader is, or wherever he reads in this volume, he will find a lift, a smile, a sense of sharing with others who have lived a day.

MAY DETHERAGE

CONTENTS

INTRODUCTION

See, I have set before thee this day life and good, and death and evil; in that I command thee this day to love the Lord thy God, to walk in his ways, and to keep his commandments and his statutes and his judgements, that thou mayest live and multiply: and the Lord thy God shall bless thee in the land whither thou goest to possess it.

—Deuteronomy 30:15-16

DAY

The *Natural* Day was from sunrise to sunset.

The *Natural* Night was from sunset to sunrise.

The *Civil* Day was from sunset one evening to sunset the next; for "the Evening and the Morning were the first day."

Night (*Ancient*)

First Watch (Lamentations 2:19) till midnight

Middle Watch (Judges 7:19) till 3 A.M.

Morning Watch (Exodus 14:24) till 6 A.M.

Day (*Ancient*)

Morning till about 10 A.M.

Heat of day till about 2 P.M.

Cool of day till about 6 P.M.

Night (*New Testament*)

First Watch, *evening*=6 to 9 P.M.
Second Watch, midnight=9 to 12 P.M.
Third Watch, cock-crow=12 to 3 A.M.
Fourth Watch, morning=3 to 6 A.M.

Day (*New Testament*)

Third hour=6 to 9 P.M.
Sixth hour=9 to 12 midday
Ninth hour=12 to 3 P.M.
Twelfth hour=3 to 6 P.M.
　　　—The Oxford Cyclopedic Concordance

A DAY

What does it take to make a day?
A lot of love along the way:
It takes a morning and a noon,
A father's voice, a mother's croon;
It takes some task to challenge all
The powers that a man may call
His own: the powers of mind and limb;
A whispered word of love; a hymn
Of hope—a comrade's cheer—
A baby's laughter and a tear;
It takes a dream, a hope, a cry
Of need from some soul passing by;
A sense of brotherhood and love;
A purpose sent from God above;
It takes a sunset in the sky,
The stars of night, the winds that sigh;
It takes a breath of scented air,
A mother's kiss, a baby's prayer.
That is what it takes to make a day:
A lot of love along the way.

　　　　　　　—William L. Stidger

14

PART I
DAWN

THE DAWN

Dawn, dew-drenched, fresh and un-trampled, comes as the Morning Star departs and the Sun stretches teasing fingers of light out to awaken the smallest living things.

Man Child early becomes aware of the world of wonderment about him. He is curious. He is delighted. He begins his explorations and with each small achievement moves on to another finding.

—*May Detherage*

Day!
Faster and more fast,
O'er night's brim, day boils at last:
Boils, pure gold, o'er the cloud-cup's brim
Where spurting and suppressed it lay,
For not a froth-flake touched the rim
Of yonder gap in the solid gray
Of the eastern cloud, an hour away;
But forth one wavelet, then another curled,
Till the whole sunrise, not to be sup-
    pressed,
Rose, reddened, and its seething breast
Flickered in bounds, grew gold,
            then overflowed the world.

—*Robert Browning, from*
            "Pippa Passes"

GLADNESS

The year's at the spring,
And day's at the morn;
Morning's at seven;
The hill-side's dew-pearled;
The lark's on the wing;
The snail's on the thorn;
God's in His Heaven—
All's right with the world!

—*Robert Browning, from*
            "Pippa Passes"

DAWN

An angel, robed in spotless white,
Bent down and kissed the sleeping Night.
Night woke to blush; the sprite was gone.
Men saw the blush and called it Dawn.

—*Paul Laurence Dunbar*

16

discovery

"WHO HAS SEEN THE WIND?"

Who has seen the wind?
  Neither I nor you:
But when the leaves hang trembling,
  The wind is passing through.

Who has seen the wind?
  Neither you nor I:
But when the trees bow down their heads,
  The wind is passing by.

—*Christina Rossetti*

THE STAR

Twinkle, twinkle, little star,
How I wonder what you are,
Up above the world so high,
Like a diamond in the sky.

. . . .

As your bright and tiny spark
Lights the traveler in the dark,
Though I know not what you are,
Twinkle, twinkle, little star.

—*Jane Taylor*

I'm glad the sky is painted blue,
And earth is painted green,
With such a lot of nice fresh air
All sandwiched in between.

—*Nursery Rhyme*

One day, with life and heart,
Is more than time enough to find a world.

—*James Russell Lowell,* "Columbus"

THIS IS MY FATHER'S WORLD

This is my Father's world;
And to my listening ears,
All nature sings, and round me rings
The music of the spheres.·
This is my Father's world;
I rest me in the thought
Of rocks and trees, of skies and seas,
His hand the wonders wrought.

This is my Father's world;
Oh, let me ne'er forget
That though the wrong seems oft so strong,
God is the ruler yet.
This is my Father's world;
Why should my heart be sad?
The Lord is king: let the heavens ring!
God reigns: let the earth be glad.

—*Maltbie D. Babcock*

A voice of greeting from the wind was
  sent,
The mists enfolded me with soft white
  arms,
The birds did sing to lap me in content,
The rivers wove their charms,
And every little daisy in the grass
Did look up in my face, and smile to see
  me pass.

—*R. H. Stoddard,* "Hymn to the
Beautiful"

For every evil under the sun,
There is a remedy, or there is none.
If there be one, try and find it;
If there be none, never mind it.

—*Nursery Rhyme*

LITTLE THINGS

Little drops of water,
  Little grains of sand,
Make the mighty ocean
  And the pleasant land.

So the little moments,
  Humble though they be,
Make the mighty ages
  Of eternity.

So our little errors
  Lead the soul away
From the path of virtue,
  Far in sin to stray.

Little deeds of kindness,
  Little words of love,
Help make earth happy
  Like the heaven above.

—*Julia Carney*

BE STRONG

Be strong!
We are not here to play, to dream, to drift.
We have hard work to do, and loads to lift.
Shun not the struggle—face it; 'tis God's
  gift.

Be strong!
Say not, "The days are evil. Who's to
  blame?"
And fold the hands and acquiesce—oh,
  shame!
Stand up, speak out, and bravely in God's
  name.

Be strong!
It matters not how deep entrenched the
  wrong,
How hard the battle goes, the day how
  long.
Faint not—fight on! Tomorrow comes the
  song.

—*Maltbie D. Babcock*

FROM THE BAREFOOT BOY

Blessings on thee, little man,
Barefoot boy, with cheek of tan!
With thy turned-up pantaloons,
And thy merry whistled tunes;
With thy red lip, redder still
Kissed by strawberries on the hill;
With the sunshine on thy face,
Through thy torn brim's jaunty grace;
From my heart I give thee joy,—
I was once a barefoot boy!
Prince thou art,—the grown-up man
Only is republican.
Let the million-dollared ride!
Barefoot, trudging at his side,
Thou hast more than he can buy
In the reach of ear and eye,—
Outward sunshine, inward joy:
Blessings on thee, barefoot boy!

—*John Greenleaf Whittier*

Thirty days hath September,
April, June, and November;
All the rest have thirty-one;
Except February, alone
Which has four and twenty-four
And every fourth year, one day more.

—*Nursery Rhyme*

It is a profound mistake to think that everything has been discovered; as well think
the horizon the boundary of the world.

—*A. M. Lemierre*

20

make believe

THE LAND OF COUNTERPANE

When I was sick and lay a-bed,
I had two pillows at my head,
And all my toys beside me lay
To keep me happy all the day.

And sometimes for an hour or so
I watched my leaden soldiers go,
With different uniforms and drills,
Among the bed-clothes, through the hills;

And sometimes sent my ships in fleets
All up and down among the sheets;
Or brought my trees and houses out,
And planted cities all about.

I was the giant great and still
That sits upon the pillow-hill,
And sees before him, dale and plain,
The pleasant land of counterpane.

—*Robert Louis Stevenson*

THE SWING

How do you like to go up in a swing,
  Up in the air so blue?
"Oh, I do think it is the pleasantest thing
  Ever a child can do!"

"Up in the air and over the wall,
  Till I can see so wide,
Rivers and trees and cattle and all
  Over the countryside—

"Till I look down on the garden green
  Down on the roof so brown—
Up in the air I go flying again,
  Up in the air and down!"

—*Robert Louis Stevenson*

MY INSIDE SELF

My Inside-Self and my Outside-Self
  Are different as can be,
My Outside-Self wears gingham smocks,
  And very round is she,
With freckles sprinked on her nose,
  And smoothly parted hair,
And clumsy feet that cannot dance
  In heavy shoes and square.

But, oh, my little Inside-Self—
  In gown of misty rose
She dances lighter than a leaf
  On blithe and twinkling toes;
Her hair is blowing gold, and if
  You chanced her face to see,
You would not think she could belong
  To staid and sober me!

—*Rachel Field*

THE INVISIBLE PLAYMATE

When the other children go,
  Though there's no one seems to see
And there's no one seems to know,
  Fanny comes and plays with me.

She has yellow curly hair
  And her dress is always blue,
And she always plays quite fair
  Everything I tell her to.

People say she isn't there—
  They step over her at play
And they sit down in her chair
  In the very rudest way.

It is queer they cannot know
  When she's there for me to see!
When the other children go
  Fanny comes and plays with me.

—*Margaret Widdemer*

From breakfast on through all the day
At home among my friends I stay;
But every night I go abroad
Afar into the land of Nod.

All by myself I have to go,
With none to tell me what to do—
All alone beside the streams
And up the mountain-sides of dreams.

The strangest things are there for me,
Both things to eat and things to see,
And many frightening sights abroad
Till morning in the land of Nod.

Try as I like to find the way,
I never can get back by day,
Nor can remember plain and clear
The curious music that I hear.

—*Robert Louis Stevenson,*
from "Land of Nod"

Our revels now are ended. These our actors,
As I foretold you, were all spirits, and
Are melted into air, into thin air;
And, like the baseless fabric of this vision,
The cloud-capp'd towers, the gorgeous
    palaces,
The solemn temples, the great globe itself,
Yea, all which it inherit, shall dissolve;
And, like this insubstantial pageant faded.
Leave not a rack behind. We are such stuff
As dreams are made on, and our little life
Is rounded with a sleep.

—*William Shakespeare,*
from The Tempest

THE FROST SPIRIT

He comes,—he comes,—the Frost Spirit
    comes!
  You may trace his footsteps now
On the naked woods and the blasted fields
    and
    the brown hill's withered brow.
He has smitten the leaves of the gray old
    trees
    where their pleasant green came forth,
And the winds, which follow wherever he
    goes,
    have shaken them down to earth.

—*John Greenleaf Whittier*

FOLLOW THE GLEAM

Not of the sunlight,
Not of the moonlight,
Not of the starlight,
O young Mariner,
Down to the haven,
Call your companions,
Launch your vessel,
And crowd your canvas,
And, ere it vanishes
Over the margin,
After, follow it,
Follow the Gleam.

—*Alfred Tennyson*

The morn is up again, the dewy morn,
with breath all incense, and with cheek
all bloom, laughing the clouds away
with playful scorn, and glowing into day.

—*Lord Byron*

belonging

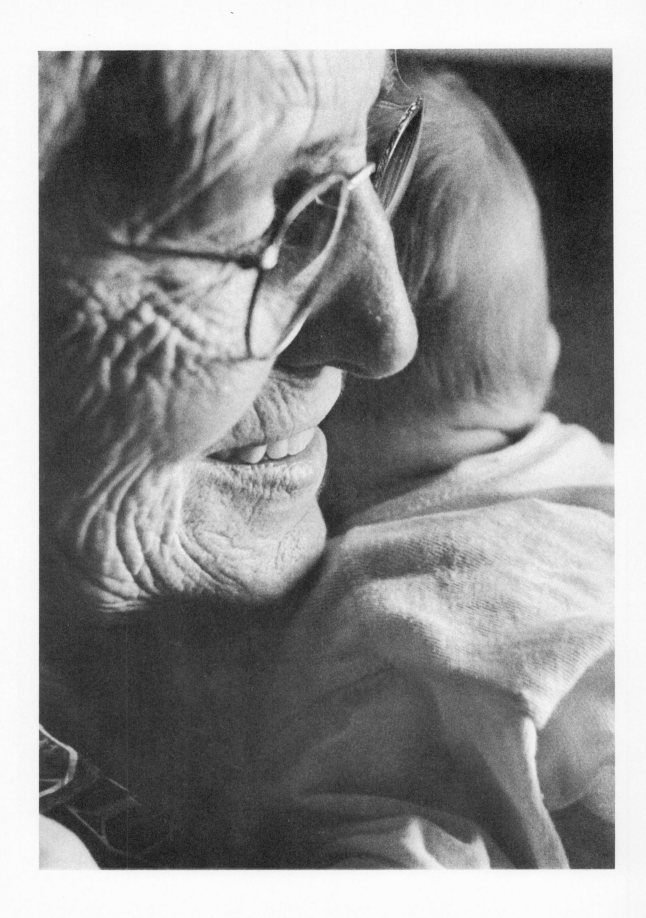

LULLABY

Sweet and low, sweet and low,
  Wind of the western sea,
Low, low, breathe and blow,
  Wind of the western sea!
Over the rolling waters go,
Come from the dying moon, and blow,
  Blow him again to me;
While my little one, while my pretty one,
    sleeps.

Sleep and rest, sleep and rest,
  Father will come to thee soon;
Rest, rest, on mother's breast,
  Father will come to thee soon;
Father will come to his bird in the nest;
Silver sails all out of the west
  Under the silver moon:
Sleep, my little one, sleep, my pretty one,
    sleep.

—Alfred Tennyson

The instruction received at the mother's knee, and the paternal lessons, together with the pious and sweet souvenirs of the fireside, are never entirely effaced from the soul.

—Lamennais

NOW I LAY ME DOWN TO SLEEP

Now I lay me down to sleep,
I pray thee, Lord, my soul to keep;
If I should die before I wake,
I pray thee, Lord, my soul to take.

—Traditional Child's Prayer

MARY'S LAMB

Mary had a little lamb,
  Its fleece was white as snow,
And every where that Mary went
  The lamb was sure to go;
He followed her to school one day—
  That was against the rule,
It made the children laugh and play,
  To see a lamb at school.

And so the Teacher turned him out,
  But still he lingered near,
And waited patiently about,
  Till Mary did appear;
And then he ran to her, and laid
  His head upon her arm,
As if he said—"I'm not afraid—
  You'll keep me from all harm."

"What makes the lamb love Mary so?"
  The eager children cry—
"O, Mary loves the lamb, you know,"
  The Teacher did reply;—
"And you each gentle animal
  In confidence may bind,
And make them follow at your call,
  If you are always kind."

—Sarah Josepha Hale

The mother's heart is the child's school-room.

—Henry Ward Beecher

Train up a child in the way he should go: and when he is old, he will not depart from it.

—Proverbs 22:6

THE GIFT

I want to give you something, my child, for we are drifting in the stream of the world.

Our lives will be carried apart, and our love forgotten.

But I am not so foolish as to hope that I could buy your heart with my gifts.

Young is your life, your path long, and you drink the love we bring you at one draught and turn and run away from us.

You have your play and your playmates. What harm is there if you have no time or thought for us?

We, indeed, have leisure enough in old age to count the days that are past, to cherish in our hearts what our hands have lost for ever.

The river runs swift with a song, breaking through all barriers. But the mountain stays and remembers, and follows her with his love.

—*Rabindranath Tagore*

MY SONG

This song of mine will wind its music around you, my child, like the fond arms of love.

This song of mine will touch your forehead like a kiss of blessing.

When you are alone it will sit by your side and whisper in your ear, when you are in the crowd it will fence you about with aloofness.

My song will be like a pair of wings to your dreams, it will transport your heart to the verge of the unknown.

It will be like the faithful star overhead when dark night is over your road.

My song will sit in the pupils of your eyes, and will carry your sight into the heart of things.

And when my voice is silent in death, my song will speak in your living heart.

—*Rabindranath Tagore*

Even a child is known by his doings, whether his work be pure, and whether it be right.

—*Proverbs 20:11*

Keep fear out of your child's mind, as you would keep poison out of his body; for fear is the deadliest of mental poisons.

—*O. S. Marden, from*
Conquest of Worry

Ships that pass in the night, and speak each
    to the other in passing,
Only a signal shown, and a distant voice in
    the darkness.
So on the ocean of life we pass and speak on
    another,
Only a look and a voice, then darkness
    again and a silence.

—*Henry Wadsworth Longfellow,*
from "A Wayside Inn"

Say to mothers, what a holy charge is theirs, with what a kingly power their love might rule the fountains of the new-born mind.

—*Lydia Sigourney*

PART II
MORNING

MORNING

Morning, sunlight and dust, and time enough before a long day ends.

Man Youth dares more in his adventures. He walks farther. He meets people. He learns more. He feels at once half-grown and then full-grown. He shakes off restraints. He decides his way and picks up his tools. He knows the Dawn, takes the Morning, and looks toward high Noon.

—*May Detherage*

My son, forget not my law; but let thine heart keep my commandments; for length of days, and long life, and peace, shall they add to thee. Let not mercy and truth forsake thee: bind them about thy neck; write them upon the table of thine heart: so shalt thou find favour and good understanding in the sight of God and man.

—*Proverbs 3:1-4*

Now the bright morning-star, Day's harbinger,
Comes dancing from the East, and leads with her
The flowery May, who from her green lap throws
The yellow cowslip and the pale primrose.
  Hail, bounteous May, that dost inspire
  Mirth, and youth, and warm desire!
  Woods and groves are of thy dressing;
  Hill and dale doth boast thy blessing.
Thus we salute thee with our early song,
And welcome thee, and wish thee long.

—*John Milton*

ALTARS

Let every corner of this day
Become an altar, Lord, for Thee,
A quiet place where I can pray
And hear Thee talk to me.

The bright expectancy of dawn
Will not endure the noonday heat,
Unless refreshing strength is drawn
Where altars touch Thy feet.

—*Sybil Armes*

aspirations

ON THE FEELING
OF IMMORTALITY IN YOUTH

No young man believes he shall ever die. There is a feeling of Eternity in youth which makes amends for everything. To be young is to be one of the Immortals.

—*William Hazlitt*

The habit of forever looking backward is fatal to efficiency just as is the habit of looking forward too much. To-day is the day. Live the day and have done with it. Fling your best into it, then you have nothing to regret, and there is no need of anticipating to-morrow.

—*O. S. Marden, from*
Conquest of Worry

A well ordered life is like climbing a tower; the view halfway up is better than the view from the base, and it steadily becomes finer as the horizon expands.

—*William Lyon Phelps*

THREE BUILDERS

"What are you doing?" a man asked of three laborers beside a building under construction.

The first man replied, "Stone-cuttin'."

The second smiled, "Puttin' in time—until a better job comes along."

The third man waited a moment and then said simply, "I'm building a cathedral!"

—*Anonymous*

Maximum Christianity means that each says to his Master:

"The most I can do is the least I can afford to do;

the most I can be is the least I can afford to be;

the most I can give is the least I can afford to give;

the most I can sacrifice is the least I can afford to sacrifice;

the most I can suffer is the least I can afford to suffer for my fellow man and for thee."

—*Frank H. Leavell, from*
Master's Minority

THE BOY SCOUT LAWS

1. A Scout is trustworthy.
2. A Scout is loyal.
3. A Scout is helpful.
4. A Scout is friendly.
5. A Scout is courteous.
6. A Scout is kind.
7. A Scout is obedient.
8. A Scout is cheerful.
9. A Scout is thrifty.
10. A Scout is brave.
11. A Scout is clean.
12. A Scout is reverent.

The Lord God is my strength, and he will make my feet like hinds' feet, and he will make me to walk upon mine high places.

—*Habakkuk 3:19*

AWARENESS

God—let me be aware.
Let me not stumble blindly down the ways,
Just getting somehow safely through the
    days,
Not even groping for another hand,
Not even wondering why it all was
    planned,
Eyes to the ground unseeking for the light,
Soul never aching for a wild-winged flight,
Please, keep me eager just to do my share.
God—let me be aware.

God—let me be aware.
Stab my soul fiercely with others' pain,
Let me walk seeing horror and stain.
Let my hands, groping, find other hands.
Give me the heart that divines, under-
    stands.
Give me the courage, wounded, to fight.
Flood me with knowledge, drench me in
    light.
Please—keep me eager just to do my share.
God—let me be aware.

—*Miriam Teichner*

Our Father which art in heaven
Hallowed be thy name.
Thy kingdom come.
Thy will be done in earth, as it is in heaven.
Give us this day our daily bread.
And forgive us our debts, as we forgive
    our debtors.
And lead us not into temptation, but de-
    liver us from evil:
For thine is the kingdom, and the power,
    and the glory, for ever. Amen.

—*Matthew 6:9-13*

We ask four things for a woman—that virtue dwell in her heart, modesty in her forehead, sweetness in her mouth, and labor in
her hands.

—*Chinese Proverb*

THE FOOTPATH TO PEACE

To be glad of life because it gives you the
chance to love and to work and to play
and to look up at the stars.

To be satisfied with your possessions,
but not contented with yourself until you
have made the best of them.

To despise nothing in the world except
falsehood and meanness and to fear nothing except cowardice.

To be governed by your admirations
rather than by your disgusts.

To covet nothing that is your neighbor's
except his kindness of heart, and gentleness
of manner.

To think seldom of your enemies, often
of your friends and every day of Christ.

And to spend as much time as you can
with body and with spirit in God's out-of-
doors.

These are little guideposts on the foot-
path to peace.

—*Henry van Dyke*

Resolved, to live with all my might while
I do live.

—*Jonathan Edwards*

BEN FRANKLIN'S LIST OF VIRTUES

1. Temperance. Eat not to dullness; drink not to elevation.
2. Silence. Speak not but what may benefit others or yourself; avoid trifling conversation.
3. Order. Let all your things have their places; let each part of your business have its time.
4. Resolution. Resolve to perform what you ought; perform without fail what you resolve.
5. Frugality. Make no expense but to do good to others or yourself; *i.e.,* waste nothing.
6. Industry. Lose no time; be always employed in something useful; cut off all unnecessary actions.
7. Sincerity. Use no hurtful deceit; think innocently and justly, and, if you speak, speak accordingly.
8. Justice. Wrong none by doing injuries, or omitting the benefits that are your duty.
9. Moderation. Avoid extremes; forbear resenting injuries so much as you think they deserve.
10. Cleanliness. Tolerate no uncleanliness in body, clothes, or habitation.
11. Tranquility. Be not disturbed at trifles, or at accidents common or unavoidable.
12. Chastity. Rarely use venery but for health or offspring, never to dullness, weakness, or the injury of your own or another's peace or reputation.
13. Humility. Imitate Jesus and Socrates.

The most beautiful works of all art were done in youth.

—*John Ruskin*

The world's interests are, under God, in the hands of the young.

—*John Trumbull*

TO MAKE THIS LIFE WORTH WHILE

May every soul that touches mine—
Be it the slightest contact—
Get therefrom some good;
Some little grace; one kindly thought;
One aspiration yet unfelt;
One bit of courage
For the darkening sky;
One gleam of faith
To brave the thickening ills of life;
One glimpse of brighter skies
Beyond the gathering mists—
To make this life worth while
And heaven a surer heritage.

—*George Eliot*

Almost every thing that is great has been done by youth.

—*Benjamin Disraeli*

I CAN

So nigh is grandeur to our dust,
So near is God to man,
When Duty whispers low, *Thou must,*
The youth replies, *I can.*

—*Ralph Waldo Emerson,*
Voluntaries, III

ST. FRANCIS' PRAYER

Lord, make me an instrument of Thy
  peace.
Where there is hate, may I bring love;
Where offense, may I bring pardon;
May I bring union in place of discord;
Truth, replacing error;
Faith, where once there was doubt;
Hope, for despair;
Light, where was darkness;
Joy to replace sadness.
Make me not to so crave to be loved as to
  love.
Help me to learn that in giving I may re-
  ceive;
In forgetting self, I may find life eternal.

—*Francis of Assisi*

Hope springs eternal in the human breast:
Man never is, but always to be, blest.

Know then thyself, presume not God to
  scan;
The proper study of mankind is man.

The same ambition can destroy or save,
And makes a patriot as it makes a knave.

Honor and shame from no condition rise;
Act well your part, there all the honor lies.

—*Alexander Pope, from* Essay on Man

Equipped? Why, the poorest young man is
equipped as only the God of the whole universe could afford to equip him.

—*Thomas DeWitt Talmadge*

Hitch your wagon to a star, but hold your
horses.

—*Ralph Waldo Emerson, from*
Civilization

"The history of heroes is the history of
the young," said Lord Beaconsfield.

Here are some—

At sixteen, Victor Hugo was writing ac-
ceptably.

At seventeen, Leigh Hunt was a prolific
writer of verse.

At eighteen, Charles H. Spurgeon was a
successful pastor; and Alexander Hamilton
commanded the attention of his country.

At nineteen, Stevenson carried in his
head a well developed steam engine; Washington Irving delighted the readers of the
Morning Chronicle; Bryant had written
"Thanatopsis"; Joan of Arc had led her
country to a lasting victory; Washington
was a major.

At twenty, Zwingli had read the New
Testament until he doubted the authority
of the "church." King Alfred had begun
one of the greatest reigns in England.

At twenty-one, Alexander had mounted
the throne.

At twenty-two Savonarola had robed
himself with a great name.

At thirty-three, Christ had descended
from the Father, had completed the plan
of salvation for mankind, had died, been
buried, had risen from the grave, and had
ascended to the right hand of the Father.

—*Frank H. Leavell, from*
Master's Minority

A SONG OF GREATNESS

When I hear the old men
Telling of heroes,
Telling of great deeds
Of ancient days,
When I hear them telling,
Then I think within me
I too am one of these.

When I hear the people
Praising great ones,
Then I know that I too
Shall be esteemed,
I too when my time comes
Shall do mightily.

—Mary Austin, tr.,
A Chippewa Indian Song

TODAY AND TOMORROW

Part of to-day belongs to to-morrow, as the seed belongs to the shoot, as the foundation belongs to the building. So to-day owes its best to to-morrow, for not to do right to-day may ruin to-morrow. But the reverse is not true. To-morrow cannot ruin to-day. Time's wheel does not run backward. Banish, then, foreboding and anxious forecast, and fill to-day with faithful work, with kindness and courage and hope; and so you will keep to-morrow from being a marplot, and make it a good, honest to-day when it comes.

—Maltbie D. Babcock

THE BOY SCOUT OATH

On my honor I will do my best—
   To do my duty to God and my country,
      and to obey the Scout law;
   To help other people at all times;
   To keep myself physically strong, mentally awake, and morally straight.

It is not necessary to live,
   But to carve our names beyond that point,
This is necessary.

—Gabriele d'Annunzio

Heaven is not reached at a single bound;
   But we build the ladder by which we rise
   From lowly earth to vaulted skies,
And we mount to its summit round by
   round.

—J. G. Holland, from "Gradatim"

God give me hills to climb,
And strength for the climbing.

—Arthur Guiterman, from "Hills"

An aspiration is a joy for ever, a possession as solid as a landed estate, a fortune which we can never exhaust and which gives us year by year a revenue of pleasurable activity. To have many of these is to be spiritually rich.

—El Dorado

For mortal daring nothing is too high.
In our blind folly we storm heaven itself.

—Horace Odes

IKE WALTON'S PRAYER

I crave, dear Lord,
No boundless hoard
  Of gold and fear,
    Nor jewels fine,
      Nor lands, nor kine,
Nor treasure heaps of anything.—
    Let but a little hut be mine
Where at the hearthstone I may hear
    The cricket sing,
      And have the shine
    Of one glad woman's eyes to make,
  For my poor sake,
      Our simple home a place divine;—
Just the wee cot—the cricket's chirr—
Love, and the smiling face of her.

    I pray not for
      Great riches, nor
For vast estates and castle-halls,—
Give me to hear the bare footfalls
      Of children o'er
        An oaken floor
New rinsed with sunshine, or bespread
With but the tiny coverlet
And pillow for the baby's head;
And, pray Thou, may
The door stand open and the day
    Send ever in a gentle breeze,
      With fragrance from the locust trees,
        And drowsy moan of doves, and blur
Of robin-chirps, and drone of bees,
      With afterhush of the stir
      Of intermingling sounds, and then
        The goodwife and the smile of her
      Filling the silences again—
          The cricket's call,
            And the wee cot,
          Dear Lord of all.
          Deny me not!

      I pray not that
      Men tremble at
        My power of place
          And lordly sway,—

I only pray for simple grace
To look my neighbor in the face
      Full honestly from day to day—
    Yield me his horny palm to hold,
      And I'll not pray
        For gold;—
The tanned face, garlanded with mirth,
It hath the kingliest smile on earth—
The swart brow, diamonded with sweat,
Hath never need of coronet.
      And so I reach,
        Dear Lord, to Thee,
      And do beseech
        Thou givest me
The wee cot, and the cricket's chirr,
Love, and the glad sweet face of her!

—*James Whitcomb Riley*

We are not to make the ideas of contentment and aspiration quarrel, for God made
them fast friends. A man may aspire, and
yet be quite content until it is time to rise;
and both flying and resting are but parts
of one contentment. The very fruit of the
gospel is aspiration. It is to the heart what
spring is to the earth, making every root,
and bud, and bough desire to be more.

—*Henry Ward Beecher*

Be a bold, brave, true, honest man. If you
know a thing is right, do it. If you have a
solemn conviction, dare to utter it in the
fear of God, regardless of the wrath of man.

—*John B. Gough*

learning

THOUGHT

I have said that the elevation of man is to be sought, or, rather, consists, first, in Force of Thought excerted for the acquisition of truth; and to this I ask your serious attention. Thought, thought, is the fundamental distinction of mind and the great work of life. All that a man does outwardly is but the expression and completion of his inward thought. To work effectually, he must think clearly. To act nobly, he must think nobly. Intellectual force is a principal element of the soul's life, and should be proposed by every man as a principal end of his being.

—*William Ellery Channing*

Born in an age and country in which knowledge and opportunity abound as never before, how can you sit with folded hands, asking God's aid in work for which He has already given you the necessary faculties and strength? Even when the Chosen People supposed their progress checked by the Red Sea, and their leader paused for Divine help, the Lord said, "Wherefore criest thou unto me? Speak unto the children of Israel, *that they go forward.*"

—*O. S. Marden, from*
Pushing to the Front

There are four chief obstacles in grasping truth, which hinder every man, however learned, and scarcely allow anyone to win a clear title to learning, namely,
—submission to faulty and unworthy authority,
—influence of custom, popular prejudice,
—concealment of our own ignorance, accompanied by
—an ostentatious display of our knowledge.

—*Roger Bacon*

It is true that we shall not be able to reach perfection, but in our struggle toward it we shall strengthen our characters and give stability to our ideas, so that, whilst ever advancing calmly in the same direction, we shall be rendered capable of applying the faculties with which we have been gifted to the best possible account.

—*Confucius*

A little learning is a dangerous thing.
Drink deep, or taste not the Pierian spring:
There shallow draughts intoxicate the
    brain,
And drinking largely sobers us again.

—*Alexander Pope, from*
Essay on Criticism

Delightful task! to rear the tender thought,
To teach the young idea how to shoot,
To pour the fresh instruction o'er the mind,
To breathe the enliv'ning spirit, and to fix
The generous purpose in the glowing
    breast.

—*James Thomson, from* "Seasons"

Young men! let the nobleness of your mind impel you to its improvement. You are too strong to be defeated, save by yourselves. Refuse to live merely to eat and sleep. Brutes can do these but you are men. Act the part of men. Prepare yourselves to endure toil. Resolve to rise; you have but to resolve. Nothing can hinder your success if you determine to succeed. Do not waste your time by wishing and dreaming, but go earnestly to work. Let nothing discourage you. If you have but little time, improve that little; if you have no books, borrow them; if you have no teachers, teach yourself; if your early education has been neglected, by the greater diligence repair the defect. Let not a craven heart or a love of ease rob you of the inestimable benefit of self-culture. Labor faithfully, labor fearlessly, and look to God, who giveth wisdom and upbraideth not, and you shall reap a harvest more valuable than gold or jewels.

—*W. D. Howard*

God always perfects his works from an elementary commencement by a regular method, and through succession of time. That is, he works by fixed law, and for this there appears this wise and benevolent reason, that is God should exercise his infinite power any otherwise, his working would be perfectly inscrutable to his intelligent creatures, and therefore to them a revelation of his power merely, and not of his wisdom.

—*A. A. Hodge*

COMMON SENSE

The excellent John Brown of Haddington, had, at times, classes of young men studying for the ministry. To one of these classes he is reported as saying: "Young gentlemen, you have come here to study theology, and to qualify yourselves for the work of the sacred ministry. And for it you need three things: First, you need grace, I hope you have it; but if not, the Lord can give it to you. Second, you need learning; and if you will study hard, I will help you get it. And, third, you need common sense; and if you haven't got that, neither I, nor the Lord can give it to you!"

—*Tryon Edwards, from* The Family Treasury

That most valuable faculty of intellectual man, the judgment, the enlightened, impartial, unbiased judgment must be kept in perpetual activity, not only in order to ascertain that the cause be good, but to determine the degree of importance in any given case, that we may not blindly assign an undue value to an inferior good.

—*Hannah More*

Prejudices, it is well known, are most difficult to eradicate from the heart whose soil has never been loosened or fertilized by education; they grow there, firm as weeds among stones.

—*Charlotte Bronte, from* Jane Eyre

BEATITUDES

Blessed are the poor in spirit: for theirs is the kingdom of heaven.

Blessed are they that mourn: for they shall be comforted.

Blessed are the meek: for they shall inherit the earth.

Blessed are they which do hunger and thirst after righteousness: for they shall be filled.

Blessed are the merciful: for they shall obtain mercy.

Blessed are the pure in heart: for they shall see God.

Blessed are the peacemakers: for they shall be called the children of God.

Blessed are they which are persecuted for righteousness' sake: for theirs is the kingdom of heaven.

Blessed are ye, when men shall revile you, and persecute you, and shall say all manner of evil against you falsely, for my sake. Rejoice, and be exceedingly glad: for great is your reward in heaven.

—Matthew 5:3-12

The more a man knows, the more he forgives.

—Anonymous

Men must be taught as if you taught them not,
And things unknown propos'd as things forgot.

—Alexander Pope, from
Essay on Criticism

Learning, though it is useful when we know how to make right use of it, yet considered as in our own power, and to those who trust to it without seeking a superior guidance, is usually the source of perplexity, strife, skepticism, and infidelity. It is, indeed, like a sword in a madman's hands, which gives him the more opportunity of hurting himself than others.

—John Newton

To know where you can find a thing is in reality the best of learning.

—Unknown

Instruction ends in the school-room, but education ends only with life. A child is given to the universe to educate.

—F. W. Robertson

I went to the woods because I wished to live deliberately, to front only the essential facts of life, and see if I could not learn what it had to teach, and not, when I came to die, discover that I had not lived.

—Henry David Thoreau

It becomes essential to choose one's path. Life consists in making these choices. One develops by choosing. It requires strength to become a child of God. . . .

In the heart of the God of the universe, each child of his is as necessary to him as the fingers are to the hand. In the marvelous design of the universe, not even a sparrow can fall to the earth meaninglessly. . . .

It is not enough to have ideals. We must translate them into action. We must clear our own little corner of creation.

—Toyohiko Kagawa, from
Meditations on the Cross

No great advance has ever been made in science, politics, or religion without controversy.

—Lyman Beecher

The vastness of the visible universe, so far as it actually comes within our means of knowledge, may be taken as a sort of image of the vastness of that range of intellectual and moral existence of which the visible universe is the platform.

—Isaac Taylor

To be fossilized is to be stagnant, unprogressive, dead, frozen into a solid. It is only "liquid currents" of thought that move men and the world.

—Wendell Phillips

The greatest men are the simplest.

—Unknown

If a man empties his purse into his head, no man can take it away from him. An investment in knowledge always pays the best interest.

—Benjamin Franklin

I keep six honest serving-men
   (They taught me all I know) ;
Their names are What and Why and When
  And How and Where and Who.

—Rudyard Kipling, from
"The Elephant's Child"

Immensity is made up of atoms.

—Leibnitz

44

self-regard

THE ACORN

I pluck an acorn from the greensward, and hold it to my ear; and this is what it says to me: "By and by the birds will come and rest in me. By and by I will furnish shade for the cattle. By and by I will provide warmth for the home in the pleasant fire. By and by I will be shelter from the storm to those who have gone under the roof. By and by I will be the strong ribs of the great vessel, and the tempest will beat against me in vain while I carry men across the Atlantic." "O foolish little acorn, wilt thou be all this?" I ask. And the acorn answers, "Yes, God and I."

—Lyman Abbott

I once asked a great man noted for his cheerfulness how he managed to keep himself so happy, and he replied that it was by not allowing himself to anticipate the misfortunes which might come to him. He always expected the best, and when unpleasant things came he made the best of them. He tried to see the ludicrous even in mishaps.

—O. S. Marden, from
Conquest of Worry

I was once very shy, but it was not long before I made two very useful discoveries: first, that all mankind were not solely employed in observing me; and next, that shamming was of no use; that the world was very clear-sighted, and soon estimated a man at his true value. This cured me.

—Sydney Smith

Oh! conscience! conscience! man's most faithful friend.
Him canst thou comfort, ease, relieve, defend:
But if he will thy friendly checks forego,
Thou are, oh! woe for me, his deadliest foe!

—George Crabbe, from
"Struggles of Conscience"

He is strong who conquers others; he who conquers himself is mighty.

—Lao-tzu

Above all things, reverence yourself.

—Pythagoras

ROOTS AND FRUITS

We are not created in Christ Jesus out of good works, but unto good works. We do not make ourselves Christians any more than we make ourselves human beings. Works are the fruit of the life, not the root. The works of the flesh are uncleanness, hatred and their bad train; the fruit of the spirit is love, joy and their good train. Life works from root to fruit: logic argues from fruit to root. We grow from our roots; we are known by our fruits.

—Maltbie D. Babcock

CONSCIENCE AND REMORSE

"Goodbye," I said to my conscience—
  "Goodbye for aye and aye,"
And I put her hands off harshly,
  And turned my face away;
And conscience smitten sorely
  Returned not from that day.

But a time came when my spirit
  Grew weary of its pace;
And I cried: "Come back, my conscience;
  I long to see thy face."
But conscience cried: "I cannot;
  Remorse sits in my place."

—*Paul Laurence Dunbar*

The reverence of man's self is, next to religion, the chiefest bridle of all vices.

—*Francis Bacon*

He that respects himself is safe from others;
He wears a coat of mail that none can
  pierce.

—*Henry Wadsworth Longfellow, from*
"Michael Angelo"

My apple trees will never get across
And eat the cones under his pines, I tell
  him.
He only says, "Good fences make good
  neighbors."

—*Robert Frost, from* "Mending Wall"

Take care that your profession does not
outrun your possession. Artificiality and hy-
pocrisy tear character to shreds eventually.

—*Maltbie D. Babcock*

The best way out is always through.

—*Robert Frost, from*
"A Servant to Servants"

Self-respect,—that corner-stone of all virtue.

—*John Herschel*

This above all: to thine own self be true,
And it must follow, as the night the day,
Thou canst not then be false to any man.

—*William Shakespeare, from* Hamlet

Self-distrust is the cause of most of our
failures. In the assurance of strength there
is strength, and they are the weakest, however strong, who have no faith in themselves or their powers.

—*Bovee*

CONSCIENTIOUSNESS

Although there is nothing so bad for conscience as trifling, there is nothing so good for conscience as trifles. Its certain discipline and development are related to the smallest things. Conscience, like gravitation, takes hold of atoms. Nothing is morally indifferent. Conscience must reign in manners as well as morals, in amusements as well as work. He only who is "faithful in that which is least" is dependable in all the world.

—*Maltbie D. Babcock*

Humility is the part of wisdom, and is most becoming in men, but let no one discourage self-reliance; it is, of all the rest, the greatest quality of true manliness."

—*Louis Kossuth*

The reflect action of transgression on the mind is spiritual blindness, on the heart, spiritual hardness, and on the will, spiritual bondage.

—*A. A. Hodge*

I will not say that it has never been done, but I am certain that a good deal of energy spent by some devout and upright people on trying to understand themselves and their motives would be expended to better purpose, and with far fuller attainment even in regard to that object itself, in the endeavor to understand God, and what He would have us do.

—*George Macdonald*

Nothing can work me damage, except myself; the harm that I sustain I carry about with me, and never am a real sufferer but by my own faults.

—*St. Bernard*

Be a friend to yersel, and ithers will.

—*Scotch Proverb*

The king is the man who can.

—*Thomas Carlyle*

As many faults come from our not esteeming ourselves enough, as from esteeming ourselves too much.

—*Charles de Secondat Montesquieu*

There is one knowledge which it is every man's duty and interest to acquire, namely, self-knowledge. Else to what end was man alone, of all animals, endued by the Creator with the faculty of self-consciousness?

The precept, "Know yourself," was not solely intended to obviate the pride of mankind; but likewise that we might understand our own worth.

—*Cicero*

A DREAM WITHIN A DREAM

Take this kiss upon the brow!
And, in parting from you now,
Thus much let me avow—
You are not wrong, who deem
That my days have been a dream.
Yet if hope has flown away
In a night, or in a day,
In a vision, or in none,
Is it therefore the less gone?
All that we see or seem
Is but a dream within a dream.

I stand amid the roar
Of a surf-tormented shore,
And I hold within my hand
Grains of the golden sand—
How few! yet how they creep
Through my fingers to the deep,
While I weep—while I weep!
O God! can I not grasp
Them with a tighter clasp?
O God! can I not save
One from the pitiless wave?
Is all that we see or seem
But a dream within a dream?

—*Edgar Allan Poe*

Nothing will make us so charitable and tender to the faults of others, as, by self-examination, thoroughly to know our own.

—*Francis de S. Fenelon*

I am better born than to be a slave to my body.

—*Seneca*

Many of our cares are but morbid ways of looking at our privileges.

—*Walter Scott*

He who appoints himself his own teacher, sends a pupil to a fool.

—*St. Bernard*

We can esteem nothing aright until we know ourselves.

—*St. Bernard*

There are different kinds of self-love. As an instinct, it is desirable and important. As a modification of true benevolence, it is commendable. But as an idolatrous affection, it is censurable.

—*C. Simmons*

Self-reverence, self-knowledge, self-control, these three alone lead life to sovereign power.

—*Alfred Tennyson*

time

MY TIME

I have no time for Envy. Straight ahead
  I see the golden path of my desire—
But Envy's ways are strange; her slaves are
    led
  Astray until they sink into the mire.

I have no time for Anger. Free, my eyes
  See clear and true, and help me on my
    way!
But Anger clouds their sight; her cruel
    lies
  Obscure the beauty of my perfect day.

I have no time for Worry. Fear would hold
  My feet, and make me stiff and halt and
    lame!
But free I travel where my path is gold,
  And all may see the road by which I
    came!

But I have time for Love, and time for
  Play—
  Yes, all the time there is, is mine to use;
And I have time for Work. I plan my day
  For these alone, yes, these alone I choose!

—Helen Cowles LeCron

Journalism is literature in a hurry.

—Matthew Arnold

Who cannot but see oftentimes how strange the threads of our destiny run? Oft it is only for a moment the favorable instant is presented. We miss it, and months and years are lost.

—Unknown

Lose this day by loitering—'t will be the same story to-morrow, and the next more dilatory.

—Unknown

John Q. Adams was never known to be behind time. The Speaker of the House of Representatives knew when to call the House to order by seeing Mr. Adams coming to his seat. Once a member said that it was time to begin. "No," said another, "Mr. Adams is not in his seat." It was found that the clock was three minutes fast, and prompt to the minute, Mr. Adams arrived.

—O. S. Marden, from
Pushing to the Front

Let's take the instant by the forward top.

—William Shakespeare

We live in deeds, not years; in thoughts, not
  breaths;
In feelings, not in figures on a dial.
We should count time by heart-throbs. He
  most lives
Who thinks most, feels the noblest, acts the
  best.

—Philip James Bailey, from "Festus"

OPPORTUNITIES

Opportunities do not come with their values stamped upon them. Everyone must be challenged. A day dawns, quite like other days; in it a single hour comes, quite like other hours; but in that day and in that hour the chance of a lifetime faces us. To face every opportunity of life thoughtfully and ask its meaning bravely and earnestly, is the only way to meet the supreme opportunities when they come, whether open-faced or disguised.

—*Maltbie D. Babcock*

I long for a life of more leisure.
I rush through the day, till it feels
As if I am chasing tomorrow
While yesterday snaps at my heels.

—*Rebecca McCann, from*
Cheerful Cherub

If you would be pungent, be brief; for it is with words as with sunbeams—the more they are condensed, the deeper they burn.

—*Robert Southey*

Believe me when I tell you that thrift of time will repay you in after life, with a usury of profit beyond your most sanguine dreams, and that waste of it will make you dwindle alike in intellectual and moral stature, beyond your darkest reckoning.

—*William E. Gladstone*

If a man has no regard for the time of other men, why should he have for their money? What is the difference between taking a man's hour and taking his five dollars?

—*Horace Greeley*

Words are like leaves, and where they most abound,
Much Fruit of sense beneath is rarely found.

—*Alexander Pope*

Brevity is the best recommendation of speech, whether in a senator or an orator.

—*Cicero*

Dost thou love life? Then do not squander time, for that is the stuff life is made of.

—*Benjamin Franklin*

Punctuality is the soul of business, as brevity of wit.

—*O. S. Marden, from*
Pushing to the Front

Time is the little grey man who takes out his breastpocket first a pocketbook, then a Dolland telescope, then a Turkey carpet, then four saddled and bridled nags and a sumptuous canvas tent. We are accustomed to chemistry and it does not surprise us. But chemistry is but a name for changes and developments as wonderful as those of this Breast-Pocket.

I was a chubby boy trundling a hoop in Chauncy Place and spouting poetry from Scott and Campbell at the Latin School, But Time, the little grey man, has taken out of his vest pocket, a great awkward house (in a corner of which I sit down and write of him), some acres of land, several full-grown and several very young persons, and seated them close beside me; then he has taken that chubbiness and that hoop quite away (to be sure he has left the declamation and the poetry), and here left a long, lean person threatening to be a little grey man, like himself.

—*Ralph Waldo Emerson*

I saw one excellency was within my reach —it was brevity, and I determined to obtain it.

—*John Jay*

With time and patience the mulberry leaf becomes satin.

—*Oriental Proverb*

Promptness is the mother of confidence and gives credit.

—*O. S. Marden, from*
Pushing to the Front

Periunt et imputantur,—the hours perish and are laid to our charge.

—*Inscription on a Dial at Oxford*

On the great clock of time there is but one word—NOW.

—*Unknown*

Truth has no special time of its own. Its hour is now—always.

—*Albert Schweitzer*

The mill cannot grind with the water that has passed.

—*O. S. Marden, from*
Conquest of Worry

TODAY

The best thing you have in this world is Today. Today is your savior; it is often crucified between two thieves, Yesterday and Tomorrow.

Today you can be happy, not yesterday or borrowed from tomorrow. There is no happiness except Today's.

Most of our misery is left over from Yesterday or borrowed from Tomorrow. Keep Today clean. Make up your mind to enjoy your food, your work, your play Today anyhow. . . .

Today is yours. God has given it to you. All your Yesterdays He has taken back. All your Tomorrows are still in His hands.

Today is yours. Take its pleasures and be glad. Take its pains and play the man. . . .

Today is yours. Use it so that at its close you can say:

I have lived, and loved, Today!

—*Frank Crane*

Brevity is very good
When we are, or are not, understood.

—*Samuel Butler*

There is more to life than increasing its speed.

—*Mahatma Gandhi*

We always have time enough, if we use it aright.

—*Goethe*

By the street of by and by one arrives at the house of never.

—*Cervantes*

Eternity itself cannot restore the loss struck from the minute.

—*Ancient Poet*

I wasted time, and now doth time waste me.

—*William Shakespeare*

God, who is liberal in all his other gifts, shows us, by the wise economy of his providence, how circumspect we ought to be in the management of our time, for he never gives two moments together.

—*Francis de S. Fenelon*

He that lacks time to mourn, lacks time to mend.
Eternity mourns that. 'Tis an ill cure
For life's worst ills, to have no time to feel them.

—*Henry Taylor, from*
Philip Van Artevelde

discipline

NO

No is next to the shortest word in the English language.

It is a concentrated declaration of independence of the human soul.

It is the central citadel of character and can remain impregnable forever.

It is the only path to reformation.

It is the steam gauge of strength, the barometer of temperament, the electric indicator of moral force.

It is an automatic safety-first device.

It has served more women than all the knights of chivalry. . . .

It is the thick wall of the home, keeping the father from folly, the mother from indiscretion, the boys from ruin, and the girls from shame.

It is the one word you can always say when you can't think of anything else.

It is the one answer that needs no explanation. . . .

The value of any Yes you utter is measured by the number of Noes banked behind it.

Live your own life. Make your own resolutions. Mark out your own program. Aim at your own mark. Determine your own conduct.

—Frank Crane

Difficulty, my brethren, is the nurse of greatness—a harsh nurse, who roughly rocks her foster children into strength and athletic proportion. The mind, grappling with great aims and wrestling with mighty impediments, grows by a certain necessity to their stature.

—William Cullen Bryant

Being at the mercy of one's disposition, a victim of one's moods, has led to some of the most frightful tragedies, and caused some of the most pitiable failures in life.

—O. S. Marden, from
Conquest of Worry

The desire of power in excess caused the angels to fall; the desire of knowledge in excess caused man to fall; but in charity is not excess, neither can man or angels come into danger by it.

—Francis Bacon, "Of Goodness"

We have to pay for everything.
Each reckless joy the spirit wills
Goes past—and then along comes life
Relentlessly collecting bills.

—Rebecca McCann, from
Cheerful Cherub

In vain do they talk of happiness who never subdued an impulse in obedience to a principle. He who never sacrificed a present to a future good, or a personal to a general one, can speak of happiness only as the blind do of colors.

—Horace Mann

FRIEND NECESSITY

What a friend Necessity is! It stops our standing on one foot, it ends our looking at our watches, and wondering about three or four things; it moves the previous question; it says, "This one thing you do." It is good discipline to conquer indecision, but it is better for us and the world, knowing "what must be," to be about it. Goethe spoke of the "dear must." Emerson calls a man's task his life-preserver. Let us recognize the purpose of God in the inevitable, and accept it gracefully, whether discipline or duty. Swift adjustment means peace and power. Necessity will then be but the iron band inside the golden crown.

—Maltbie D. Babcock

THE DRAMA OF HUMAN STRUGGLE

Job went through every test the human spirit is heir to, and he was victorious. The seven tests of Job's life:

1. The test of prosperity
2. The test of adversity
3. The test of sorrow
4. The test of physical affliction
5. The test of domestic infelicity
6. Intellectual tests
7. Spiritual tests

—Dean Dutton, from
Quests and Conquests

Self-control is the very essence of character.

—O. S. Marden, from
Conquest of Worry

He that plants thorns must never expect to gather roses.

—Pilpay (Bidpai),
"The Ignorant Physician"

One of the most important, but one of the most difficult things for a powerful mind is, to be its own master.

—Joseph Addison

When the wind is rising it is good for each ship at sea to look to its own ropes and sails, and not stand gazing to see how ready the other ships are to meet it.

—Phillips Brooks

If we were to see a person mired in a swamp, desperately struggling to extricate himself, would we not run to his rescue without hesitation? We would certainly not add to his danger by pushing him in deeper. But somehow, when a person is angered, instead of trying to help him put out the fire of his passion by our own calmness, helping him to neutralize it, we only add fuel to the flames by flying into a passion ourselves.

—O. S. Marden, from
Conquest of Worry

Adversity is the trial of principle. Without it a man hardly knows whether he is honest or not.

—*Henry Fielding*

Prosperity is no just scale; adversity is the only balance to weigh friends.

—*Plutarch*

The heights by great men reached and kept
Were not attained by sudden flight,
But they, while their companions slept,
Were toiling upward in the night.

—*Henry Wadsworth Longfellow, from*
"The Ladder of St. Augustine"

When our hatred is too keen, it places us beneath those we hate.

—*Frances Rochefoucauld*

God holds you responsible for your nature plus your nurture, for yourself plus your possibilities.

—*Maltbie D. Babcock*

I'll not willingly offend,
    Nor be easily offended:
What's amiss I'll strive to mend,
    And endure what can't be mended.

—*Isaac Watts from "Good Resolutions"*

No man is justified in doing evil on the ground of expediency.

—*Theodore Roosevelt, from*
"The Strenuous Life"

Felicity, not fluency of language, is a merit.

—*E. P. Whipple*

Liberality consists rather in giving seasonably than much.

—*Jean de La Bruyere*

A man must stand erect, not be kept erect by others.

—*Marcus Aurelius*

61

When we have practiced good actions awhile, they become easy; when they are easy, we take pleasure in them; when they please us we do them frequently; and then, by frequency of act, they grow into a habit.

—*Archbishop Tillotson*

My appetite for life is large.
I want adventures far away,
Yet leave untasted half the time
The humbler joys of everyday.

—*Rebecca McCann, from*
Cheerful Cherub

Oh, what tangled web we weave,
When first we practise to deceive!

—*Walter Scott, from* "Marmion"

I mean to make myself a man, and if I succeed in that, I shall succeed in everything else.

—*James A. Garfield*

A man can never be a true gentleman in manner until he is a true gentleman at heart.

—*Charles Dickens*

There are two freedoms, the false where one is free to do what he likes, and the true where one is free to do what he ought.

—*C. Kingsley*

O! beware, my lord, of jealousy;
It is the green-eyed monster, which doth
   mock
The meat it feeds on.

—*William Shakespeare, from* Othello

A man must first govern himself ere he is fit to govern a family; and his family ere he is fit to bear the government of the commonwealth.

—*Sir Walter Raleigh*

Do today thy nearest duty.

—*Goethe*

A laugh is worth a thousand groans in the market.

—*Charles Lamb*

actions

SOMEBODY'S MOTHER

The woman was old and ragged and gray
And bent with the chill of the Winter's day.

The street was wet with a recent snow,
And the woman's feet were aged and slow.

She stood at the crossing and waited long,
Alone, uncared for, amid the throng

Of human beings who passed her by
Nor heeded the glance of her anxious eye.

Down the street, with laughter and shout,
Glad in the freedom of "school let out,"

Came the boys like a flock of sheep,
Hailing the snow piled white and deep;

Past the woman so old and gray
Hastened the children on their way;

Nor offered a helping hand to her—
So meek, so timid, afraid to stir

Lest the carriage wheels or the horses' feet
Should crowd her down in the slippery
street.

At last one came of the merry troop,
The gayest laddie of all the group;

He paused beside her and whispered low,
"I'll help you cross, if you wish to go."

Her aged hands on his strong young arm
She placed, and so, without hurt or harm,

He guided the trembling feet along,
Proud that his own were firm and strong.

Then back again to his friends he went,
His young heart happy and well content.

"She's somebody's mother, boys, you know,
For all she's aged, and poor, and slow,

"And I hope some fellow will lend a hand
To help my mother, you understand,

"If ever she's poor and old and gray,
When her own dear boy is far away."

And "somebody's mother" bowed low her
head
In her home that night, and the prayer she
said

Was, "God be kind to the noble boy,
Who is somebody's son, and pride and joy!"

—*Mary Dow Brine*

The art of using moderate abilities to advantage wins praise, and often acquires more reputation than actual brilliancy.

—*Frances Rochefoucauld*

An obstinate man does not hold opinions, but they hold him; for when he is once possessed with an error, it is like a devil, only cast out with great difficulty. He delights most of all to differ in things indifferent. He is resolved to understand no man's reason but his own, because he finds no man can understand his but himself. His opinions are like plants that grow upon rocks, that stick fast though they have no rooting. The more inconsistent his views are, the faster he holds them, otherwise they would fall asunder of themselves; for opinions that are false ought to be held with more strictness than those that are true, otherwise they will be apt to betray their owners before they are aware.

—*Bishop Butler*

Politeness has been compared to an air cushion, which, although there is apparently nothing in it, eases our jolts wonderfully.

—*George L. Carey*

A FAREWELL

My fairest child, I have no song to give you;
   No lark could pipe to skies so dull and
      grey:
Yet, ere we part, one lesson I can leave you
   For every day.

Be good, sweet maid, and let who will be
      clever;
   Do noble things, not dream them, all
      day long:
And so make life, death, and that vast for-
      ever
   One grand, sweet song.

—*Charles Kingsley*

The love principle is stronger than the force principle.

—*A. A. Hodge*

We do not what we ought,
   What we ought not, we do;
And lean upon the thought
   That chance will bring us through.

—*Matthew Arnold*

The boy who has acquired a reputation for punctuality has made the first contribution to the capital that in after years makes his success a certainty.

—*Heywood Campbell Brown*

Anger at another's fault
I cannot honestly condone—
It's nearly always just a way
We turn attention from our own.

—*Rebecca McCann, from*
    Cheerful Cherub

Birth's gude, but breedin's better.

—*Scotch Proverb*

Eat at your own table as you would eat at the table of the king.

—*Confucius*

The great secret, Eliza, is not having bad manners or good manners or any particular sort of manners, but having the same manner for all human souls: in short, behaving as if you were in Heaven, where there are no third-class carriages, and one soul is as good as another.

—*George Bernard Shaw, from*
    Pygmalion

Don't dally with your purpose.

—*O. S. Marden, from*
Pushing to the Front

FORGIVENESS

How sure we are of our own forgiveness from God. How certain we are that we made in his image, when we forgive heartily and out of hand one who has wronged us. Sentimentally we may feel, and lightly we may say, "To err is human, to forgive is divine"; but we never taste the nobility and divinity of forgiving till we forgive and know the victory of forgiveness over our sense of being wronged, over mortified pride and wounded sensibilities. Here we are in living touch with Him who treats us as though nothing had happened—Who turns his back upon the past and bids us journey with Him into goodness and gladness, into newness of life.

—*Maltbie D. Babcock*

Conduct is three fourths of life.

—*Matthew Arnold*

A profound conviction raises a man above the feeling of ridicule.

—*John Stuart Mill*

A centipede was happy quite
   Until a frog in fun
Said, "Pray, which leg comes after which?"
This raised her mind to such a pitch,
She lay distracted in the ditch
   Considering how to run.

—*Anonymous*

Men's proper business in this world falls mainly into three divisions:
1. To know themselves and the existing state of things they have to do with.
2. To be happy in themselves and the existing state of things.
3. To mend themselves and the existing state of things, as far as either are marred or mendable. Now men, reverse all this. We have a general readiness to take delight in anything past, future, far off, or somewhere else, rather than in anything now, or near, or here, leading us gradually to place our pleasures principally in the exercise of the imagination, and to build all our satisfactions upon things as they are not.

—*John Ruskin*

I rush to bargain counters.
I will not be impeded.
I find such wild strange objects
I never knew I needed.

—*Rebecca McCann, from*
Cheerful Cherub

PRAYER

Forgive us, Lord Jesus, for doing the things that make us uncomfortable and guilty when we pray.

We say that we believe in God, and yet we doubt God's promises.

We say that in God we trust, yet we worry and try to manage our own affairs.

We say that we love Thee, O Lord, and yet do not obey Thee.

We believe that Thou has the answers to all our problems, and yet we do not consult Thee.

Forgive us, Lord, for our lack of faith and the wilful pride that ignores the way, the truth, and the life.

Will Thou reach down and change the gears within us that we may go forward with Thee. Amen.

—*Peter Marshall*

As a nation we are intolerant of rest. If we have a brilliant man, we insist upon him always shining. We want our rose bushes to bloom all the year round, we would have our trees all bearing fruit, and our suns always shining. We kill three-fourths of our truly great men in the prime of life by expecting and exacting too much of them, and then call the legitimate result of our forcing system a dispensation of Providence. Like the earth, minds must lie fallow at times. Perpetual crops will exhaust any soil, and perpetual excitement will wear out any mind or body.

—*Waverly Magazine*

If your mind is saturated with fear, worry, discouragement, hatred, envy, jealousy, it has no room for the nobler emotions.

—*O. S. Marden, from*
Conquest of Worry

Our religion should be carried into everything. It should go with us to the farm and the factory; to the counting house and the court house; into the sick chamber not only, but into the senate chamber; with the mariner it should ride the stormy sea, and with the miner it should descend into the bowels of the earth; it should sit with the artist in his studio, with the teacher in his school room, with the lawyer in his office; it should go with the physician to his patients and the artisan to his shop; it should stand with the salesman behind the counter and with the clerk at his desk; it should be carried into our pleasures, and by no means be absent from our politics.

—*W. D. Howard*

Nothing will stunt one's growth, and starve and strangle his vitality, like living in the constant atmosphere of worry.

—*O. S. Marden, from*
Conquest of Worry

Truth makes life a noble thing,
And courage makes it strong,
But grace and tact must set them off
As music does a song.

—*Rebecca McCann, from*
Cheerful Cherub

friendship

FRIENDLY TALK

But after all, the very best thing is good talk, and the thing that helps it most, is friendship. How it dissolves the barriers that divide us, and loosens all constraints and diffuses itself like some fine old cordial through all the veins of life—this feeling that we understand and trust each other, and wish each other heartily well. Everything into which it really comes is good. It transforms letter-writing from a task into a pleasure. It makes music a thousand times more sweet. The people who play and sing not at us but to us, how delightful it is to listen to them! Yes, there is a talkability that can express itself even without words. There is an exchange of thoughts and feeling which is happy alike in speech and in silence. It is quietness pervaded with friendship.

—*Henry van Dyke*

Doing nothing for others is the undoing of one's self. We must be purposely kind and generous, or we miss the best part of existence. The heart that goes out of itself, gets large and full of joy. This is the great secret of the inner life. We do ourselves the most good doing something for others.

—*Horace Mann*

Our lives all interweave,
Each needed in its place.
And every heavy heart
Is weighing down the race.

—*Rebecca McCann, from*
Cheerful Cherub

The happiness of love is in action; its test is what one is willing to do for others.

—*Lew Wallace*

You'll never hope
To be such friends, for instance, she and you,
As when you hunted cowslips in the woods,
Or played together in the meadow hay.
Oh yes—with age, respect comes, and your worth
Is felt, there's growing sympathy of tastes,
There's ripened friendship, there's confirmed esteem.

—*Robert Browning, from*
A Blot in the 'Scutcheon

Some tears fell down my cheeks and then I smiled,
As those smile who have no face in the world
To smile back to them. I had lost a friend.

—*Elizabeth Barrett Browning, from*
"Aurora Leigh"

Judge not thy friend until thou standest in his place.

—*Rabbi Hillel*

TO A FRIEND

I love you not only for what you are, but for what I am when I am with you.

I love you not only for what you have made of yourself, but for what you are making of me.

I love you for the part of me that you bring out.

I love you for putting your hand into my heaped-up heart and passing over all the foolish and the frivolous and weak things that you can't help dimly seeing there, and for drawing out into light all the beautiful radiant belongings that no one else had looked quite far enough to find.

I love you for ignoring the possibilities of the fool and weakling in me, and for laying firm hold on the possibilities of the good in me.

I love you for closing your ears to the discords in me, and for adding to the music in me by worshipful listening.

I love you because you are helping me to make of the timber of my life, not a tavern, but a temple, and of the words of my every day not a reproach, but a song.

I love you because you have done more than any creed could have done to make me happy.

You have done it without a touch, without a word, without a sign.

You have done it at first, by being yourself.

After all, perhaps this is what being a friend means.

—*Unknown*

Friendship is to be purchased only by friendship.

—*Thomas Wilson*

Thick waters show no images of things;
Friends are each other's mirrors, and should be
Clearer than crystal, or the mountain springs,
And free from clouds, design, or flattery.
For vulgar souls no part of friendship share;
Poets and friends are born to what they are.

—*Catherine Philips, "Friendship"*

A friend you have to buy won't be worth what you pay for him, no matter what that be.

—*G. D. Prentice*

Tell me whom you admire, and I will tell you what you are.

—*O. S. Marden, from* Pushing to the Front

Nobody who is afraid of laughing, and heartily too, at his friend, can be said to have a true and thorough love for him; and on the other hand, it would betray a sorry want of faith to distrust a friend because he laughs at you. Few men are much worth loving in whom there is not something well worth laughing at.

—*Guesses at Truth*

FRIENDSHIP LASTS

If stores of dry and learned lore we gain
We keep them in the memory of the
  brain;
Names, things, facts—whatever we knowl-
  edge call,
There is the common ledger for them all;
And images on this cold surface traced
Make slight impression and are soon ef-
  faced.
But we've a page more glowing and more
  bright
On which our friendship and our love to
  write;
That these may never from the soul depart,
We trust them to the memory of the heart.
There is no dimming—no effacement here;
Each pulsation keeps the record clear;
Warm golden letters all the tablet fill,
Nor lose their luster till the heart stands
  still.

     —Daniel Webster

Blessed are they who have the gift of making friends, for it is one of God's best gifts.
It involves many things, but above all, the
power of going out of oneself and seeing
and appreciating whatever is noble and
loving in another.

     —Thomas Hughes

A friend to chide me when I'm wrong,
 My inmost soul to see;
And that my friendship prove as strong
 For him as his for me.

     —John Quincy Adams

I try to be friends with the whole human
  race
And feel they're my brothers whatever they
  do,
Except those at concerts who sit next to me
And put on their rubbers before it's all
  through.

     —Rebecca McCann, from
     Cheerful Cherub

Ah, how good it feels!
The hand of an old friend.

  —Henry Wadsworth Longfellow, from
     "John Endicott"

Honest men esteem and value nothing so
much in this world as a real friend. Such
a one is as it were another self, to whom
we impart our most secret thoughts, who
partakes of our joy, and comforts us in our
affliction; add to this, that his company is
an everlasting pleasure to us.

     —Pilpay (Bidpai)

What is a friend? I will tell you. It is a
person with whom you dare to be yourself.

     —Frank Crane, from
     "A Definition of Friendship"

SONGS IN ABSENCE

Were you with me, or I with you,
There's nought, methinks, I might not do;
Could venture here, and venture there,
And never fear, nor ever care.

To things before, and things behind,
Could turn my thoughts, and turn my
    mind,
On this and that, day after day,
Could dare to throw myself away.

Secure, when all was o'er, to find
My proper thought, my perfect mind,
And unimpaired receive anew
My own, and better self in you.

—*Clough*

If a man does not make new acquaintances as he passes through life, he will soon find himself left alone. A man should keep his friendship in constant repair.

—*Samuel Johnson*

Every book is, in an intimate sense, a circular letter to the friends of him who writes it. They alone take his meanings; they find private messages, assurances of love, and expressions of gratitude, dropped for them in every corner. The public is but a generous patron who defrays the postage.

—*Robert Louis Stevenson, from*
"*Travels with a Donkey*"

The friendship of a great man is a favor of the gods.

—*Napoleon*

The greatest happiness in life is the conviction that we are loved, loved for ourselves, or rather loved in spite of ourselves.

—*Victor Hugo*

A faithful and true friend is a living treasure, inestimable in possession, and deeply to be lamented when gone. Nothing is more common than to talk of a friend; nothing more difficult than to find one; nothing more rare than to improve by one as we ought.

A friend should be one in whose understanding and virtue we can equally confide, and whose opinion we can value at once for its justness and sincerity.

He who has made the acquisition of a judicious and sympathizing friend, may be said to have doubled his mental resources.

—*Robert Hall*

There are three faithful friends—an old wife, an old dog, and ready money.

—*Benjamin Franklin*

love

A PRAYER FOR LOVE

God, give me love; I do not only pray
  That perfect love may be bestowed on
    me;
  But let me feel the lovability
Of every soul I meet along the way.
Though it be hidden from the light of day
  And every eye but Love's. Oh! I would
    see
  My brother in the monarch and the
    bee—
In every spirit clothed in mortal clay!

Give me the gift of loving! I will claim
  No other blessing from the Lord of
    Birth,
  For he who loves needs no high-sounding
    name,
  Nor power nor treasure to proclaim his
    worth;
His soul has lit at Life's immortal flame
A lamp that may illumine all the earth.

—*Elsa Barker*

No man ever loved except by his own free
choice, nor became fully a man until he
freely chose to love.

—*Robert Raynolds, from*
  The Choice to Love

Forgiving love is a possibility only for
those who know they are not good, who
feel themselves in need of divine mercy,
who—know that the difference between the
good man and the bad man are insignificant
in God's sight.

—*Reinhold Niebuhr*

Love always looks for love again.
If ever single, it is twin,
And till it finds its counterpart
It bears about an aching heart.

—*R. H. Stoddard, from "Love's Will"*

Love does not consist in gazing at each
other (one perfect sunrise gazing at another!) but in looking outward together
in the same direction.

—*Antoine de Exupéry*

LOVER TO LOVER

Leave me a while, for you have been too
  long
A nearness that is perilous and sweet:
Loose me a little from the tightening
  thong
That binds my spirit, eyes and hands and
  feet.
For there are old communions I would
  hold,
To mind my heart what field and sky may
  be:
Earth bears her fruit . . . November has a
  gold . . .
And stars are still high points in constancy.
Loose me a little, now. . . . I have a need
Of standing in an open, windy place,
Of saying names again, of giving heed
To these companions of man's lonely
  race . . .
Loose me to these, between one dusk and
  dawn;—
I shall have need of them, when you are
  gone.

—*David Morton*

True love's the gift which God has given
To man alone beneath the heaven;
It is not fantasy's hot fire,
Whose wishes, soon as granted, fly;
It liveth not in fierce desire,
With dead desire it doth not die;
It is the secret sympathy,
The silver link, the silken tie,
Which heart to heart, and mind to mind,
In body and in soul can bind.

—*Walter Scott, from* "Lady of the Lake"

For not to love is the blackest enemy of all life, a stone of darkness in our heart.

When man stops hiding himself from God, and from that of God in another, and from that of God in himself, and says with a whole heart: "Thou hast made me. I shall face Thee," then he has chosen to love; he has chosen to meet his whole appointment with God, and the fear of death is over, and he dwells in the light of life.

The choice to love is the highest achievement of man's will, and the good hard work of loving is man's proper spiritual toil. If we do not this, all else we do is futile. If we do this we are no longer hiding from God. And the meaning of a man's life is to be a person of God.

The purpose of magic is to compel God to do our bidding. We dream that we can achieve this purpose. Love is response to God, which is very different from the dream of magic that would order Him about.

—*Robert Raynolds, from*
The Choice to Love

Christ gave us the keynote when He enjoined us to love our enemies; to love those who persecute us and abuse us. Nothing more scientific was ever uttered than that loving our enemies will cure them. It is the only thing that will do so. Speaking kindly of those who insult us, abuse us, and say unkind things about us, is the only way to thwart them. Harmony is the only cure for discord, as light is for darkness, and truth for error.

—*O. S. Marden, from*
Conquest of Worry

Love has never yet just happened to anybody. To be loved includes having chosen to accept the love offered to us; to love is a chosen act and a voluntary effort. The opportunities for love are all about us all the time; if love happened to us and fell upon us like weather, we would be drenched in it all the time; and if love were an unconscious action, like normal breathing, we would give it no more thought than we give to our breathing.

Love indeed is a chosen action, not a gift, not a feeling, not an emotion, not a mere reaction; often feelings, emotions have to be overcome in order to love; old choices of hostility have to be renounced in order to choose to love; and mere reaction to environmental stimuli have sometimes to be consciously controlled and directed in order to love.

Love is a chosen action that lifts up the quality of our life. It is a basic act of communion.

—*Robert Raynolds, from*
The Choice to Love

FOR WINDOW SHOPPERS

Should any woman come to me
And ask, love, to set you free,
I'd say, "Of course. But you understand
This love you want is second hand,
And I suppose it's only fair
To warn you that it will not wear."
Then should I meet her on the street,
I'd make her triumph less complete
By whispering loud so she could hear,
"That's my old love she's flaunting, dear."

—Elizabeth Draper

Love spends his all, and still hath store.

—Phillip James Bailey, from "Festus"

Love hurt my heart until I saw
It never could be owned by me,
But when I freely gave my love
I found it set my own heart free.

—Rebecca McCann, from
Cheerful Cherub

AT NIGHTFALL

I need so much the quiet of your love
  After the day's loud strife;
I need your calm all other things above
  After the stress of life.

I crave the haven that in your heart lies,
  After all toil is done;
I need the starshine of your heavenly eyes,
  After the day's great sun.

—Charles Hanson Towne

Some men deem
Gold their god, and esteem
Honor is the chief content
That to man in life is lent;
And some others do contend,
Quiet none like to a friend;
Others hold there is no wealth
Compared to a perfect health;
Some man's mind in quiet stands
When he is lord of many lands;
But I did sigh, and said all this
Was but a shade of perfect bliss;
And in my thoughts I did approve,
Naught so sweet as is true love.

—Robert Greene, from "Philomela's
Ode That She Sung in Her Arbor"

For love is generous in offering and generous in receiving; it is full of laughter, mercy, and rejoicing; it is just without blindfold and powerful without coercion, and sets us free by giving us our lives, not demanding them. . . . Meanwhile each man is loaded and lives with a thousand ideas that contradict one another, but a decent love for himself keeps them from destroying each other and him; and any two people may meet in the infinite watch of God and offer and accept love to and from one another. It is indeed nonsense to hide our lives in prisons of ideas, and not come forth to meet and to love.

Each of us knows that his heart is ready for the mirth and solace and dancing joy of coming forth to love. To love is the divine disturbance that gives us life.

—Robert Raynolds, from
The Choice to Love

EARTH LOVER

Old loveliness has such a way with me,
    That I am close to tears when petals fall
    And needs must hide my face behind a
        wall,
When autumn trees burn red with ecstasy.
For I am haunted by a hundred things
    And more than I have seen in April days;
    I have worn stars above my head in
        praise,
    I have worn beauty as two costly rings.

Alas, how short a state does beauty keep,
    Then let me clasp it wildly to my heart
    And hurt myself until I am a part
Of all its rapture, then turn back to sleep.
    Remembering through all the dusty
        years
    What sudden wonder brought me close
        to tears.

—Harold Vinal

POSTSCRIPT

Go! Leave me now,
My day is full,
This parting brings
No sorrow.
But, oh, my dear,
I may not have
A thing to do
Tomorrow.

—Elizabeth Draper

QUERY

I often wonder, dearest dear,
Are you faithful there as you are here?
Or from other lips do you seek wine,
Missing the familiar touch of mine?
The reason I should like to know
My conscience sometimes hurts me so!

—Elizabeth Draper

A new commandment I give unto you,
That ye love one another; as I have loved
you, that ye also love one another.

—John 13:34

The sweetest joy, the wildest woe is love.

—Phillip James Bailey, from "Festus"

WHEN THERE IS MUSIC

Whenever there is music, it is you
Who come between me and the sound of
    strings:
The cloudy portals part to let you through,
Troubled and strange with long remember-
    ings.
Your nearness gathers ghostwise down the
    room,
And through the pleading violins they
    play,
There drifts the dim and delicate perfume
That once was you, come dreamily astray.

Behind what dim and shadowy doors you
    wait
That such frail things as these should set
    you free!
When all my need, like armies at a gate,
Would storm in vain to bring you back to
    me;
When in this hush of strings you draw more
    near
Than any sound of music that I hear.

—David Morton

MY GIFT

What can I give Him
Poor as I am;
If I were a shepherd,
I would give Him a lamb.
If I were a wise man,
I would do my part.
But what can I give Him?
I will give my heart.

—Christina Rossetti

THE LOVE YOU LIBERATE

If you do not love your work there is no plainer fact in this world than this—you can't keep it long.

Liberate your love and it enters into everything you do. It enlarges your soul and strengthens your body.

And the love you liberate is the only love that ever comes back to you.

You can't get anything without giving something.

I have never met an unhappy giver.

We have to do a great many unpleasant things in this world. But if we do them in the spirit of good sports I notice that they usually are not so unpleasant after all. This love business, you see, works overtime and doesn't mind.

The love you liberate breeds greater love everywhere it goes. It's contagious. In the long run it travels around the world.

If you are working for an organization and you try merely to "just get by," your position itself shrinks and you with it. Love then scampers to the fellow above or below you who puts his heart into his work and so climbs!

Life is a vast business. A part of it is given over to making people happy and a part to the making of money, building ships or planes, buildings, roads, bridges and babies' toys. All these pursuits are useful and valuable. But love is the salt that savors the whole and drives away the mists so that the sun may shine and warm.

Love is the greatest thing in the world and the most important ingredient that enters into life and work.

Liberate your love. Spread it out. Keep giving it away. Don't mind if you overflow with it aboard. If there is damage done it is easily repaired!

—George Matthew Adams

GOD KEEP YOU

God keep you, dearest, all this lonely night:
   The winds are still,
   The moon drops down behind the
      western hill;
God keep you safely, dearest, till the light.

God keep you then when slumber melts
     away,
   And cares and strife
   Take up new arms to fret our waking
     life,
God keep you through the battle of the
     day.

God keep you. Nay, beloved soul, how vain,
   How poor is prayer!
   I can but say again, and yet again,
God keep you every time and every where.

—Mary Ainge DeVere

   Love is not love
Which alters when it alteration finds,
Or bends with the remover, to remove.
O, no! It is an ever-fixed mark,
That looks on tempests and is never
   shaken.

—William Shakespeare, from
     "Sonnet 116"

WHO LOVES THE RAIN

Who loves the rain
And loves his home,
And looks on life with quiet eyes,
Him will I follow through the storm;
And at his hearth-fire keep me warm;
Nor hell nor heaven shall that soul surprise,
Who loves the rain
And loves his home,
And looks on life with quiet eyes.

—*Frances Wells Shaw*

SONG

You bound strong sandals on my feet,
You gave me bread and wine,
And sent me under sun and stars,
For all the world was mine.

Oh take the sandals off my feet,
You know not what you do;
For all my world is in your arms,
My sun and stars are you.

—*Sara Teasdale*

True love, like Greek fire, is inextinguishable.

—*Ike Marvel*

There is an atmosphere in the letters of those we love which we alone—we who love—can feel.

—*Marion Harland*

If thou must love me, let it be for nought
Except for love's sake only. Do not say
"I love her for her smile—her look—her way
Of speaking gently,—for a trick of thought
That falls in well with mine, and certes brought
A sense of pleasant ease on such a day"—
For these things in themselves, Beloved, may
Be changed, or change for thee—and love, so wrought,
May be unwrought so. Neither love me for
Thine own dear pity's wiping my cheeks dry:
A creature might forget to weep, who bore
Thy comfort long, and lose thy love thereby!
But love me for love's sake, that evermore
Thou mayst love on, through love's eternity.

—*Elizabeth Barrett Browning,*
"Sonnets from the Portuguese, XIV"

Like an island in a river
Art thou, my love, to me,
And I journey by thee ever,
With gentle ecstasy.

—*Philip James Bailey, from "Festus"*

There is never jealousy where there is not strong regard.

—*Washington Irving*

PART III
NOON

NOON

Noon. Hot high Noon. No shadow to show influence or a way to go. Sun straight up. Morning is gone. Afternoon will be too late.

Man is at the controls. He acts now. He does what he must. He is the man of this hour, and he cannot evade it. The way he came in the Morning will direct what he does, but now is his time. He carries the load. He is responsible. It is his hour.

—May Detherage

IT'S FINE TODAY

Sure, this world is full of trouble—
  I ain't said it ain't.
Lord, I've had enough and double
  Reason for complaint;
Rain and storm have come to fret me,
  Skies are often gray;
Thorns and brambles have beset me
  On the road—but say,
    Ain't it fine today?

It's today that I am livin',
  Not a month ago.
Havin'; losin'; takin'; givin';

As time wills it so.
Yesterday a cloud of sorrow
  Fell across the way.
It may rain again tomorrow,
  It may rain—but say,
    Ain't it fine today?

—Douglas Malloch

TODAY

With every rising of the sun
Think of your life as just begun.

The Past has cancelled and buried deep
All yesterdays. There let them sleep.

Concern yourself with but Today.
Grasp it, and teach it to obey

Your will and plan. Since time began
Today has been the friend of man.

You and Today! A soul sublime
And the great heritage of time.

With God himself to bind the twain,
Go forth, brave heart! Attain! Attain!

—Anonymous

commitment

AS THE MASTER WILLS

Slowly, through all the universe, the temple of God is being built. Wherever, in any world, a soul, by free-willed obedience, catches the fire of God's likeness, it is set into the growing walls, a living stone. When, in your hard fight, in your tiresome drudgery, or in your terrible temptation, you catch the purpose of your being, and give yourself to God, and so give Him the chance to give Himself to you, your life, a living stone, is taken up and set into that growing wall. Wherever souls are being tried and ripened, in whatever commonplace and homely ways;—there God is hewing out the pillars for His temple. Oh, if the stone can only have some vision of the temple of which it is to be a part forever, what patience must fill it as it feels the blows of the hammer, and knows that success for it is simply to let itself be wrought into what shape the Master wills.

—*Phillips Brooks*

THE SOUL GATHERS FORCE

It is possible, when the future is dim, when our depressed faculties can form no bright ideas of the perfection and happiness of a better world,—it is possible still to cling to the conviction of God's merciful purpose towards His creatures, of His parental goodness even in suffering; still to feel that the path of duty, though trodden with a heavy heart, leads to peace; still to be true to conscience; still to do our work, to resist temptation, to be useful, though with diminished energy, to give up our wills when we cannot rejoice under God's mysterious providence. In this patient, though uncheered obedience, we become prepared for light. The soul gathers force.

—*W. E. Channing*

In all great successes we can trace the power of concentration, riveting every faculty upon one unwavering aim; perseverance in the pursuit of an undertaking in spite of every difficulty; and courage which enables one to bear up under all trials, disappointments, and temptations.

—*O. S. Marden, from*
Pushing to the Front

MY CREED

To live as gently as I can;
To be, no matter where, a man;
To take what comes of good or ill
And cling to faith and honor still;
To do my best, and let that stand
The record of my brain and hand;
And then, should failure come to me,
Still work and hope for victory.

To have no secret place wherein
I stoop unseen to shame or sin;
To be the same when I'm alone
As when my every deed is known;
To live undaunted, unafraid
Of any step that I have made;
To be without pretense or sham
Exactly what men think I am.

To leave some simple mark behind
To keep my having lived in mind;
If enmity to aught I show,
To be an honest, generous foe,
To play my little part, nor whine
That greater honors are not mine.
This, I believe, is all I need
For my philosophy and creed.

—*Edgar A. Guest*

ON HIS BLINDNESS

When I consider how my light is spent,
Ere half my days, in this dark world and
    wide,
And that one talent which is death to hide
Lodged with me useless, though my soul
    more bent
To serve therewith my Maker, and present
My true account, lest He returning chide,
Doth God exact day-labour, light denied?
I fondly ask; but Patience, to prevent
That murmur, soon replies, God doth not
    need
Either man's work or His own gifts: who
    best
Bears his mild yoke, they serve Him best;
    His state
Is Kingly. Thousands at His bidding speed
And post o'er land and ocean without rest:
They also serve who only stand and wait.

—John Milton

DEDICATION

Dedication is only the power of making continuous efforts. The line between failure and success is so fine that we scarcely know when we pass it—so fine that we are often on the line and do not know it.

There is no failure except in no longer trying. There is no defeat except from within, no really insurmountable barrier save our own inherent weakness of purpose.

—Elbert Hubbard

Pattern after Him who gave the Golden Rule, and who was the first true gentleman that ever breathed.

—O. S. Marden, from
Pushing to the Front

The only conclusive evidence of a man's sincerity is that he gives himself for a principle. Words, money, all things else are comparatively easy to give away; but when a man makes a gift of his daily life and practice, it is plain that the truth, whatever it may be, has taken possession of him.

—James Russell Lowell

Let us beware of losing our enthusiasm. Let us ever glory in something, and strive to retain our admiration for all that would ennoble, and our interest in all that would enrich and beautify our life.

—Phillips Brooks

So in every well-balanced life, no matter how versatile in endowments or how broad in culture, there is one grand central purpose, in which all the subordinate powers of the soul are brought to a focus, and where they will find fit expression. In nature we see no waste of energy, nothing left to chance. Since the shuttle of creation shot for the first time through chaos, design has marked the course of every golden thread. Every leaf, every flower, every crystal, every atom even, has a purpose stamped upon it which unmistakably points to the crowning summit of all creation—man.

—O. S. Marden, from
Pushing to the Front

JENNY LIND'S REPLY

The Swedish Nightingale, Jenny Lind, won great success as an operatic singer, and money poured into her purse. Yet she left the stage when singing her best and never went back to it. She must have missed the money, the fame and the applause of thousands, but she was content to live in privacy.

Once an English friend found her sitting on the steps of a bathing machine on the sea sands, with a Bible on her knee, looking out into a glorious sunset. They talked and the conversation drew near to the inevitable question. "O Madame Goldschmidt, how is it that you ever came to abandon the stage at the very height of your success?"

"When, every day," was the quiet reply, "it made me think less of this [laying a finger on the Bible] and nothing at all of that [pointing at the sunset], what else could I do?"

—*Dean Dutton, from*
Quests and Conquests

FORGIVENESS

My heart was heavy, for its trust had been
Abused, its kindness answered with foul
    wrong;
So, turning gloomily from my fellow-men
One summer Sabbath day I strolled among
The green mounds of the village burial-
    place;
Where, pondering how all human love and
    hate
Find one sad level; and how, soon or late,
Wronged and wrongdoer, each with meek-
    ened face,
And cold hands folded over a still heart,
Pass the green threshold of our common
    grave,

Whither all footsteps tend, whence none
    depart,
Awed for myself, and pitying my race,
Our common sorrow, like a mighty wave,
Swept all my pride away, and trembling I
    forgave!

—*John Greenleaf Whittier*

OBEDIENCE

Men say, that when they know they will do; Jesus says, that when they do they will know. He does not promise to manifest himself to the man who dreams or debates, but to him who keeps his commandments. The seeds of truth sprout in the soil of obedience. The words of Jesus in the mind of a disobedient man are no more vital than wheat in the wrappings of a mummy. To know the divinity of Jesus' teachings, we must do his will with definite intention. Moral disobedience is mental darkness, but to submit our wills in loyalty to his law is to open our minds to the light of his truth.

—*Maltbie D. Babcock*

The longer I live, the more deeply am I convinced that that which makes the difference between one man and another— between the weak and powerful, the great and insignificant, is energy—invincible determination—a purpose once formed, and then death or victory.

—*Fowell Buxton*

Few things are impossible to diligence and skill.

—*Samuel Johnson,* Rasseles

THOROUGHBRED CODE

I believe in work. For discontent and labor are not often companions.

I believe in thrift. For to store up a little regularly is to store up character as well.

I believe in simple living. For simplicity means health and health means happiness.

I believe in loyalty. For if I am not true to others, I can not be true to myself.

I believe in a cheerful countenance. For a sour face is the sign of a grouch.

I believe in holding up my chin. For self-respect commands respect from others.

I believe in keeping up courage. For troubles flee before a brave front.

I believe in bracing up my brother. For an encouraging word may save the day for him.

I believe in living up to the best that is in me. For to lower the standard is to give up the fight.

—Calvin Coolidge

BEGIN THE DAY WITH GOD

Every morning lean thine arms awhile
Upon the window-sill of heaven
And gaze upon thy Lord.
Then, with the vision in thy heart,
Turn strong to meet thy day.

—Unknown

Impossibilities recede as experience advances.

—Arthur Helps, Friends in Council

APPROACHES

When thou turn'st away from ill,
Christ is this side of thy hill.

When thou turnest toward good,
Christ is walking in thy wood.

When thy heart says, "Father, pardon!"
Then the Lord is in thy garden.

When stern Duty wakes to watch,
Then His hand is on the latch.

But when Hope thy song doth rouse,
Then the Lord is in the house.

When to love is all thy wit,
Christ doth at thy table sit.

When God's will is thy heart's pole,
Then is Christ thy very soul.

—George Macdonald

May the outward and the inward man be at one.

—Socrates, Phraedus

And the things that thou hast heard of me among many witnesses, the same commit thou to faithful men, who shall be able to teach others also. Thou therefore endure hardness, as a good soldier of Jesus Christ. No man that warreth entangleth himself with the affairs of this life; that he may please him who hath chosen him to be a soldier. And if a man also strive for masteries, yet he is not crowned, except he strive lawfully.

—II Timothy 2:2-5

liberty

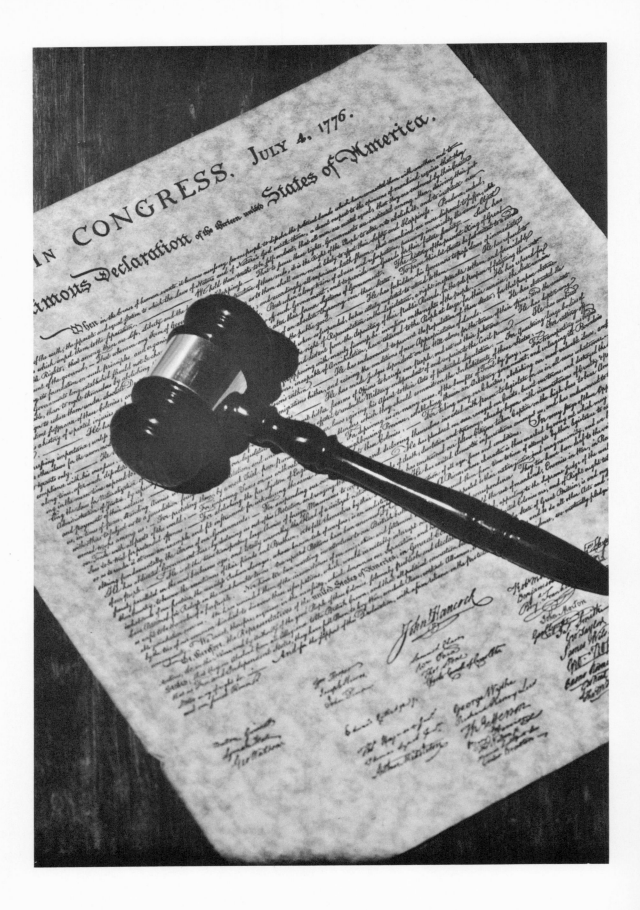

The law of liberty tends to abolish the reign of race over race, of faith over faith, of class over class. It is not the realization of a political ideal: it is the discharge of moral obligation.

—*J. E. E. Dalberg-Acton*

If [freedom] is a thing of the spirit. Men must be free to worship, to think, to hold opinions, to speak without fear. They must be free of challenge wrong and oppression with surety of justice. Freedom conceives that the mind and the spirit of man can be free only if he be free to pattern his own life, to develop his own talents, free to earn, to spend, to save, to acquire property as the security of his old age and his family.

—*Herbert C. Hoover*

Liberty is always unfinished business.

—*John Adams*

Liberty cannot be preserved without a general knowledge among the people. . . .

The preservation of the means of knowledge among the lowest ranks is of more importance to the public than all the property of all the rich men in the country.

There is but one element of government, and that is THE PEOPLE. From this element spring all governments. "For a nation to be free, it is only necessary that she wills it." For a nation to be a slave, it is only necessary that she wills it.

—*John Adams*

There is nothing so degrading as the constant anxiety about one's means of livelihood. . . . Money is like a sixth sense without which you cannot make a complete use of the other five.

—*William Somerset Maugham, from*
Of Human Bondage

Liberty is the most jealous and exacting mistress that can beguile the brain and soul of man. From him who will not give her all, she will have nothing. She knows that his pretended love serves but to betray. But when once the fierce heat of her quenchless, lustrous eyes have burned into the victim's heart, he will know no other smile but hers.

—*Clarence S. Darrow*

I would define liberty to be a power to do as we would be done by. The definition of liberty to be the power of doing whatever the law permits, meaning civil laws, does not seem satisfactory.

—*John Adams*

THE SECRET OF TRUE LIBERTY

The law of the spirit of life in Christ Jesus made me free from the law of sin and of death. Romans 8:2

That which is obvious and self-evident is frequently false and generally superficial.

It is only by striking down into the hidden depths of our nature that we come to those paradoxes in which the essence of truth resides.

"He that findeth his life shall lose it."

That is a contradiction in terms, but it is a reality in experience.

"He that is greatest among you shall be your servant."

That is a falsehood to the sense, but it is a truth to the soul.

"He only is wise who knows himself to be a fool."

To a little learning, that seems absurd, but to a profound philosophy it is the voice of wisdom.

What is liberty?

It is the recognition of voluntary allegiance to the highest law.

And what is the highest law?

It is the law of gratitude and love.

Who, then, is free?

He who sees and feels the obligations which call him to serve the highest and the best.

The noblest, richest, fullest, purest life is that which has the deepest and strongest sense of indebtedness resting upon it always, and impelling it forward along the line of duty, which is also the line of joy.

So, then, true liberty is the highest kind of bondage.

—*Henry van Dyke, from*
Six Days of the Week

No bad man is free.

—*Epictetus*

When liberty is gone,
Life grows insipid and has lost its relish.

—*Joseph Addison, from "Cato"*

Liberty and good government do not exclude each other; and there are excellent reasons why they should go together. Liberty is not a means to a higher political end. It is itself the highest political end.

—*J. E. E. Dalberg-Acton*

My whole and sole object, from first to last, from the time of putting off my leather apron to this day, has been a Free Press and Free Discussion. When I first started as a hawker of pamphlets I knew nothing of political principles, I had never read a page of Paine's writings; but I had a complete conviction that there was something wrong somewhere, and that the right application of the printing-press was the remedy.

—*Richard Carlile*

What other liberty is there worth having, if we have not freedom and peace in our minds, if our inmost and most private man is but a sour and turbid pool?

—*Henry David Thoreau*

History proves that dictatorships do not grow out of strong and successful governments, but out of weak and helpless ones. If by democratic methods people get a government strong enough to protect them from fear and starvation, their democracy succeeds; but if they do not, they grow impatient. Therefore, the only sure bulwark of continuing liberty is a government strong enough to protect the interests of the people, and a people strong enough and well enough informed to maintain its sovereign control over its government.

—*Franklin Delano Roosevelt*

The biggest and most pertinent lesson in history—at least for democracies—is that they cannot take their existence for granted.

—*Norman Cousins*

There is no freedom on earth or in any star for those who deny freedom to others.

—*Elbert Hubbard*

Liberty, like day,
Breaks on the soul, and by a flash from Heaven
Fires all the faculties with glorious joy.

—*William Cowper, from* "The Task"

A state which is incompetent to satisfy different races condemns itself; a state which does not include them is destitute of the chief basis of self-government. The theory of nationality, therefore, is a retrograde step in history.

—*J. E. E. Dalberg-Acton*

If you limit the search for truth and forbid men anywhere, in any way, to seek knowledge, you paralyze the vital force of truth itself.

In the best sense of the word, Jesus was a radical. His religion has been so long identified with conservation—often with conservatism of the obstinate and unyielding sort—that it is almost startling for us sometimes to remember that all of the conservatism of his own times was against him; that it was the young, free, restless, sanguine, progressive part of the people who flocked to him.

—*Phillips Brooks*

When a government takes over a people's economic life it becomes absolute, and when it has become absolute it destroys the arts, the minds, the liberties and the meaning of the people it governs.

—*Maxwell Anderson, from*
The Guaranteed Life

No person can be punished for entertaining or professing religious beliefs or disbeliefs, for church attendance or non-attendance.

No tax in any amount, large or small, can be levied to support any religious activities or institutions, whatever they may be called, or whatever for they may adopt to teach or practice religion.

The First Amendment has erected a wall between church and state. That wall must be kept high and impregnable. We could not approve the slightest breach.

—*Hugo L. Black*

Among a people generally corrupt, liberty cannot exist.

—*Edmund Burke*

The wish, which ages have not yet subdued In man, to have no master save his mood.

—*Lord Byron, from* "Island"

Men are free when they are in a living homeland, not when they are straying and breaking away. . . . The most unfree souls go west, and shout of freedom. Men are freest when they are most unconscious of freedom.

—*D. H. Lawrence*

War is an invention of the human mind, The human mind can invent peace with justice.

—*Norman Cousins*

Let men laugh, if they will, when you sacrifice desire to duty.—You have time and eternity to rejoice in.

—*Theodore Parker*

Liberty is always dangerous, but it is the safest thing we have.

—*Harry Emerson Fosdick*

Liberty means responsibility. That is why most men dread it.

—*George Bernard Shaw,*
Maxims for Revolutionists

There are two good things in life, freedom of thought and freedom of action.

—*William Somerset Maugham, from*
Of Human Bondage

religion

Without the Bible man would be in the midst of a sandy desert, surrounded on all sides by a dark and impenetrable horizon.

—*Daniel Webster*

The message of Jesus Christ, our Savior, is the story of the Bible—it is the story of salvation. Profound students of the Bible have traced the story of Jesus Christ from the beginning of the Old Testament, for He is the true theme of the Old as well as the New Testament.

He appears in Genesis as the Seed of the Woman.

In Exodus, He is the Passover Lamb.

In Leviticus, He is the Atoning Sacrifice.

In Numbers, He is the Smitten Rock.

In Deuteronomy, He is the Prophet.

In Joshua, He is the Captain of the Lord's Hosts.

In Judges, He is the Deliverer.

In Ruth, He is the Heavenly Kinsman.

In the six books of Kings, He is the Promised King.

In Nehemiah, He is the Restorer of the nation.

In Esther, He is the Advocate.

In Job, He is my Redeemer.

In Psalms, He is my All and in all.

In Proverbs, He is my Pattern.

In Ecclesiastes, He is my Goal.

In the Song of Solomon, He is my Satisfier.

In the Prophets, He is the Coming Prince of Peace.

In the Gospels, He is Christ coming to seek and to save.

In Acts, He is Christ risen.

In the Epistles, He is Christ at the Father's right hand.

In the Revelation, He is Christ returning and reigning.

—*Billy Graham, from* Peace with God

CREED

Shall I ask the brave soldier who fights by my side
In the cause of mankind, if our creeds agree?
Shall I give up the friend I have valued and tried,
If he kneel not before the same altar with me?

—*Thomas Moore*

ENERGY IN RELIGION

Now, of all pursuits in the world, the Christian profession requires the most energetic action, and it utterly fails where diligence and zeal are absent. What can a man do as a farmer, a merchant, a carpenter, or even a beggar, unless he follows up his calling with activity and perseverance? A sluggard desireth and hath nothing, whatever his trade may be. What, then can he hope to win who calls himself a Christian and neither learns of Christ as his teacher, follows Him as his Master, nor serves Him as his Prince? Salvation is not by works, but it is salvation from idleness. We are not saved because we are earnest; but he who is not earnest has great reason to question whether he is saved.

—*Charles Haddon Spurgeon*

WHO WAS CHRISTUS?

Who was this one of whom the ages tell,
   The lowly Peasant come from Nazareth,
   And yet who knew the words of life and
     death?
He came all hope into our earthly hell;
But men, poor dwellers in the nature-shell,
   Saw not that He had come to set them
     free:
   He was too great for their hearts: they
     could not see
He drew his water fom a higher well.

His dreams rose beautiful as builder
    towers;
And now despite the darkness of these
    hours,
   I know his will and who He is I know:
He is the Lord of songs and suns afar,
   Lord of the light and the unerring bow,
The bright Apollo of the central star.

           —*Edwin Markham*

The man with whom prayer is a habit will
soon acquire the language of prayer; and
if a minister has not this language of prayer,
this vocabulary of the Christian closet, a
congregation will do well to reject him.
They who never attend drill will appear
badly on review.

           —*Hugh Miller*

What I want is, not to possess religion,
but to have a religion that shall possess me.

           —*Charles Kingsley*

War will never yield but to the principles
of universal justice and love, and these
have no sure root but in the religion of
Jesus Christ.

        —*William Ellery Channing*

The great Easter truth is not that we are
to live newly after death—that is not the
great thing—but that we are to be new
here and now by the power of the resurrection; not so much that we are to live
forever as that we are to, and may, live
nobly now because we are to live forever.

           —*Phillips Brooks*

"He preaches well that lives well," quoth
Sancho, "that's all the divinity I can understand."

           —*Cervantes*

There are few signs in a soul's state more
alarming than that of religious indifference, that is, the spirit of thinking all religions equally true, the real meaning of
which is, that all religions are equally false.

           —*F. W. Robertson*

society

GOOD SOLDIERS

What the world needs today is not a new system of ethics.

It is simply a larger number of people who will make a steady effort to live up to the system that they have already.

There is plenty of room for heroism in the plainest kind of duty.

The greatest of all wars has been going on for centuries. It is the ceaseless, glorious conflict against the evil that is in the world.

—*Arthur Helps*

This Court acknowledges, as I suppose, the validity of the Law of God. . . . I endeavored to act up to that instruction I say, I am yet too young to understand that God is any respector of persons. I believe that to have interferred as I have done, always freely admitted I have done, in behalf of His despised poor, was not wrong, but right. Now, if it is deemed necessary that I should forfeit my life for the furtherance of the ends of justice, and mingle my blood further with the blood of my children, and with the blood of millions in this slave country whose rights are disregarded by wicked, cruel, and unjust enactments, I submit, so let it be done!

—*John Brown*

Whenever there is lost the consciousness that every man is an object of concern for us just because he is a man, civilization and morals are shaken, and the advance to folly developed in humanity is only a question of time.

—*Albert Schweitzer*

Society can progress only if men's labors show a profit—if they yield more than is put in. To produce at a loss must leave less for all to share.

—*Bernard M. Baruch*

A man that seeks truth and loves it must be reckoned precious to any human society.

—*Frederick the Great*

Never follow the crowd.

—*Bernard M. Baruch*

No race can prosper till it learns that there is as much dignity in tilling a field as in writing a poem.

—*Booker T. Washington*

The members of the human race
Who move me most to scornful diction
Are sensitive and injured souls
Luxuriating in affliction.

—*Rebecca McCann, from*
Cheerful Cherub

LIBERTY AND EQUALITY

To perfect society, it is necessary to develop the faculties, intellectual and moral, with which man is endowed. But the mainspring to their development, and through this to progress, improvement and civilization, with all their blessings, is the desire of individuals to better their condition. For this purpose liberty and security are indispensable.

—John C. Calhoun

Bees will not sting a man smeared with honey.

—O. S. Marden, from
Pushing to the Front

I live for those who love me,
  For those who know me true,
For the heaven that smiles above me,
  And awaits my spirit too;
For the cause that lacks assistance,
For the wrong that needs resistance,
For the future in the distance,
  And the good that I can do.

—G. Linnaeus Banks

All higher motives, ideals, conceptions, sentiments in a man are of no account if they do not come forward to strengthen him for the better discharge of the duties which devolve upon him in the ordinary affairs of life.

—Lyman Beecher

The true gentleman cannot harbor those qualities which excite the antagonism of others, as revenge, hatred, malice, envy, or jealousy, for those poison the sources of spiritual life and shrivel the soul. Generosity of heart and a genial good will towards all are absolutely essential to him who would possess fine manners.

—O. S. Marden, from
Pushing to the Front

A man's own good breeding is the best security against other people's ill manners. It carries along with it a dignity that is respected by the most petulant.

—Phillip Dormer Chesterfield

Genuine good taste consists in saying much in a few words, in choosing among our thoughts, in having order and arrangement in what we say, and in speaking with composure.

—Francis de S. Fenelon

Why should there not be a patient confidence in the ultimate justice of the people? Is there any better or equal hope in the world?

—Abraham Lincoln

An inevitable dualism bisects nature, so that each thing is a half, and suggests another thing to make it whole; as spirit, matter; man, woman; subjective, objective; in, out; upper, under; motion, rest; yes, nay. . . .

The same dualism underlies the nature and conditions of man. Every excess causes a defect; every defect an excess. . . . Every faculty which is a receiver of pleasure, has an equal penalty put on its abuse. . . . Nature hates monopolies and exceptions. . . .

Every secret is told, every crime is punished, every virtue rewarded, every wrong redressed, in silence and certainty.

All infractions of love and equity in our social relations are speedily punished. They are punished by Fear. While I stand in simple relations to my fellow man, I have no displeasure in meeting him.

—*Ralph Waldo Emerson, from*
"Compensation"

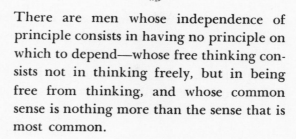

There are men whose independence of principle consists in having no principle on which to depend—whose free thinking consists not in thinking freely, but in being free from thinking, and whose common sense is nothing more than the sense that is most common.

—*M. W. Jacobus*

I never knew a man I didn't like.

—*Will Rogers*

Speech is civilization itself. The word, even the most contradictory word, preserves contact. It is silence which isolates.

—*Thomas Mann*

Words are pins, in the cushion of the tongue.
Because they are familiar and inexpensive, often I am careless in using them and fail to consider that they can prick and wound.
I must remember that they serve a useful purpose and constitute a blessing when used as they were intended—to pin together the thoughts of my life with those of others.

—*Carolyn Rhea, from*
Such Is My Confidence

Justice and truth are the common ties of society.

—*John Locke*

My political ideal is democracy. Let every man be respected as an individual and no man idolized.

—*Albert Einstein*

You must talk facts, you must name names, you must impute motives. You must say what is in your mind. . . . If you are not strong enough to face the issue in private life, do not dream that you can do anything for public affairs.

—*John Jay Chapman*

In every society where property exists there will ever be a struggle between rich and poor. Mixed in one assembly, equal laws can never be expected; they will either be made by the members to plunder the few who are rich, or by the influence to influence the many who are poor.

—*John Adams*

Semantics teach us to watch our prejudices, and to take our exercise in other ways than jumping to conclusions. Semantics is the propagandist's worst friend.

—*Stuart Chase*

Peace cannot be kept by force. It can only be achieved by understanding.

—*Albert Einstein*

Society undergoes continual changes; it is barbarous, it is civilized, it is Christianized, it is rich, it is scientific; but this change is not amelioration. For everything that is given something is taken. Society acquires new arts, and loses old instincts. The civilized man has built a coach, but has lost the use of his feet; he has a fine Geneva watch, but cannot tell the hour by the sun.

—*Ralph Waldo Emerson*

Let him who expects one class of society to prosper in the highest degree, while the other is in distress, try whether one side of his face can smile while the other is pinched.

—*Margaret Fuller*

Christian society is like a bundle of sticks laid together, whereof one kindles another. Solitary men have fewest provocations to evil, but again, fewest incitations to good. So much as doing good is better than not doing evil will I account Christian good-fellowship better than an hermitish and melancholy solitariness.

—*Joseph Hall*

Every man depends on the quantity of sense, wit, or good manners he brings into society for the reception he meets within it.

—*William Hazlitt*

work

THE COMMON TASKS

The common tasks are beautiful if we
Have eyes to see their shining ministry.
The plowman with his share deep in the
    loam;
The carpenter whose skilled hands build a
    home;
The gardener working with reluctant sod,
Faithful to his partnership with God—
These are the artisans of life. And, oh,
A woman with her eyes and cheeks aglow,
Watching a kettle, tending a scarlet flame,
Guarding a little child—there is no name
For this great ministry. But eyes are dull
That do not see that it is beautiful;
That do not see within the common tasks
The simple answer to the thing God asks
Of any child, a pride within His breast:
That at our given work we do our best.

—*Grace Noll Crowell*

I must work the works of him that sent
me, while it is day: the night cometh,
when no man can work.

—*John 9:4*

Genius is one per cent inspiration and
ninety-nine per cent perspiration.

—*Thomas Alva Edison*

The reward for work well done is more
work to do.

—*Monroe E. Dodd*

There never was a day that did not bring
its own opportunity for doing good, that
never could have been done before, and
never can be again.

—*William Henry Burleigh*

Whatever you are by nature, keep to it;
never desert your line of talent. Be what
nature intended you for, and you will
succeed; be anything else, and you will be
ten thousand times worse than nothing.

—*Sidney Smith*

WORK

If you are poor—work.
If you are rich—continue to work.
If you are burdened with seemingly unfair
    responsibilities,—work.
If you are happy—keep right on working.
    Idleness gives room for doubts and fears.
If disappointments come—work.
If sorrow threatens you and loved ones
    seem not true—work.
If health is threatened—work.
When faith falters and reason fails—just
    work.
Work as if your life is in peril. It really is.
Whatever happens or matters—work.
Work faithfully—work with faith.
Work is the greatest material remedy avail-
    able.
Work will cure both mental and physical
    afflictions.

—*Fannie A. Matthews, from*
    The Silent Partner

WORK

Work!
Thank God for the might of it,
The ardor, the urge, the delight of it—
Work that springs from the heart's desire,
Setting the brain and the soul on fire—
Oh, what is so good as the heat of it,
And what is so glad as the beat of it,
And what is so kind as the stern command,
Challenging brain and heart and hand?

Work!
Thank God for the pride of it,
For the beautiful, conquering tide of it,
Sweeping the life in its furious flood,
Thrilling the arteries, cleansing the blood,
Mastering stupor and dull despair,
Moving the dreamer to do and dare.
Oh, what is so good as the urge of it,
And what is so glad as the surge of it,
And what is so strong as the summons deep,
Rousing the torpid soul from sleep?

Work!
Thank God for the pace of it,
For the terrible, keen, swift race of it;
Fiery steeds in full control,
Nostrils a-quiver to greet the goal.
Work, the Power that drives behind,
Guiding the purposes, taming the mind,
Holding the runaway wishes back,
Reining the will to one steady track,
Speeding the energies faster, faster,
Triumphing over disaster.
Oh, what is so good as the pain of it,
And what is so great as the gain of it?
And what is so kind as the cruel goad,
Forcing us on through the rugged road?

Work!
Thank God for the swing of it,
For the clamoring, hammering ring of it,
Passion of labor daily hurled
On the mighty anvils of the world.
Oh, what is so fierce as the flame of it?

And what is so huge as the aim of it?
Thundering on through dearth and doubt,
Calling the plan of the Maker out.
Work, the Titan; Work, the friend,
Shaping the earth to a glorious end,
Draining the swamps and blasting the hills,
Doing whatever the Spirit wills—
Rending a continent apart,
To answer the dream of the Master's heart.
Thank God for a world where none may
    shirk—
Thank God for the splendor of work!

—*Angela Morgan*

WORKING WITH GOD
"My Father worketh hitherto, and I work."
And I work! Say that too. If you destroy
the sequence, life loses heart, and joy, and
meaning, and value. Swing into line with
the eternal energy, be a force among forces,
a toiler, a producer, a factor, and life never
loses its tone and flavor, its bead or glam-
our. There is no real taste to bread nor
bliss in sleep for the idler. He is the
doubter, the skeptic, the unhappy man. His
idleness proclaims him diseased and de-
caying.

—*Maltbie D. Babcock*

When you work for the thing you believe in
You're rich though the whole way is
    rough—
But work that is simply for money
Will never quite pay you enough.

—*Rebecca McCann, from*
Cheerful Cherub

NINTH BEATITUDE

There is a ninth beatitude
    that sheds its magic grace;
Blessed is the man
    who has found his place.

Blessed is the man
    whose hands are strong,
Who works with a will
    the whole day long.

Blessed is the labor
    he can do;
Blessed is his home
    when work is through.

Blessed is the soul
    that does not shirk;
Blessed is the man
    who has found his work.

—Anne Campbell

The reason why most men do not achieve more is because they do not attempt more.

—Unknown

A singular mischance has happened to some of our friends. At the instant when He ushered them into existence, God gave them a work to do, and He also gave them a competence of time; so much that if they began at the right moment, and wrought with sufficient vigor, their time and their work would end together.

—Alexander Hamilton

Labour without joy is base. Labour without sorrow is base. Sorrow without labour is base. Joy without labour is base.

—John Ruskin

Open eyes will discover opportunities everywhere; open ears will never fail to detect the cries of those who are perishing for assistance; open hearts will never want for worthy objects upon which to bestow their gifts; open hands will never lack for noble work to do.

—O. S. Marden, from
Pushing to the Front

No cheating or bargaining will ever get a single thing out of nature at half price. Do we want to be strong? We must work. To be happy? We must be kind. To be wise? We must look and think.

—John Ruskin

We must respect the work we do.
A slipshod method never pays—
It may get by, but in our minds
It makes a scar that always stays.

—Rebecca McCann, from
Cheerful Cherub

WORK

Then a ploughman said, Speak to us of Work.

And he answered, saying:

You work that you may keep pace with the earth and the soul of the earth.

For to be idle is to become a stranger unto the seasons, and to step out of life's procession, that marches in majesty and proud submission towards the infinite.

When you work you are a flute through whose heart the whispering of the hours turns to music.

Which of you would be a reed, dumb and silent, when all else sings together in unison?

Always you have been told that work is a curse and labour a misfortune.

But I say to you that when you work you fulfil a part of earth's furthest dream, assigned to you when that dream was born,

And in keeping yourself with labour you are in truth loving life,

And to love life through labour is to be intimate with life's inmost secret.

But if you in your pain call birth an affliction and the support of the flesh a curse written upon your brow, then I answer that naught but the sweat of your brow shall wash away that which is written.

You have been told also that life is darkness, and in your weariness you echo what was said by the weary.

And I say that life is indeed darkness save when there is urge,

And all urge is blind save when there is knowledge,

And all knowledge is vain save when there is work,

And all work is empty save when there is love;

And when you work with love you bind yourself to yourself, and to one another, and to God.

And what is it to work with love?

It is to weave the cloth with threads drawn from your heart, even as if your beloved were to wear that cloth.

It is to build a house with affection, even as if your beloved were to dwell in that house.

It is to sow seeds with tenderness and reap the harvest with joy, even as if your beloved were to eat the fruit.

It is to charge all things you fashion with a breath of your own spirit,

And to know that all the blessed dead are standing about you and watching.

Often have I heard you say, as if speaking in sleep, "He who works in marble, and finds the shape of his own soul in the stone, is nobler than he who ploughs the soil.

And he who seizes the rainbow to lay it on a cloth in the likeness of man, is more than he who makes the sandals for our feet."

But I say, not in sleep but in the over-wakefulness of noontide, that the wind speaks not more sweetly to the giant oaks than to the least of all the blades of grass;

And he alone is great who turns the voice of the wind into a song made sweeter by his own loving.

Work is love made visible.

And if you cannot work with love but only with distaste, it is better that you should leave your work and sit at the gate of the temple and take alms of those who work with joy.

For if you bake bread with indifference, you bake a bitter bread that feeds but half man's hunger.

And if you grudge the crushing of the grapes, your grudge distils a poison in the wine.

And if you sing though as angels, and love not the singing, you muffle man's ears to the voices of the day and the voices of the night.

—*Kahlil Gibran, from* **The Prophet**

The one prudence in life is concentration; the one evil is dissipation; and it makes no difference whether our dissipations are coarse or fine. . . . Everything is good which takes away one plaything and delusion more, and sends us home to add one stroke of faithful work.

—*Ralph Waldo Emerson*

If you want knowledge you must toil for it; and if pleasure you must toil for it. Toil is the law. Pleasure comes through toil, and not by self-indulgence and indolence. When one gets to love work, his life is a happy one.

—*John Ruskin*

If a man can write a better book, preach a better sermon, or make a better mousetrap than his neighbor, though he build his house in the woods, the world will make a beaten path to his door.

—*Ralph Waldo Emerson*

Blessed is he who found his work. Let him ask no other blessedness. He has a work— a life purpose; he has found it, and will follow it.

—*Thomas Carlyle*

Weak men wait for opportunities, strong men make them.

—*O. S. Marden, from* **Pushing to the Front**

I never did anything worth doing by accident; nor did any of my inventions come by accident; they came by work.

—*Thomas Alva Edison*

It is only those who do not know how to work that do not love it. To those who do, it is better than play—it is religion.

—*J. H. Patterson*

Work should never make me weary
If I'm really meant to do it,
But it soon becomes exhausting
If it's greed that drives me to it.

—*Rebecca McCann, from* **Cheerful Cherub**

WORK

Let me but do my work from day to day,
  In field or forest, at the desk or loom,
  In roaring market-place or tranquil
    room;
Let me but find it in my heart to say,
When vagrant wishes beckon me astray,
  "This is my work; my blessing, not my
    doom;
  Of all who live, I am the one by whom
This work can best be done in the right
    way."

Then shall I see it not too great, nor small,
  To suit my spirit and to prove my
    powers;
  Then shall I cheerful greet the laboring
    hours,
And cheerful turn, when the long shadows
    fall
At eventide, to play and love and rest,
Because I know for me my work is best.

              —Henry van Dyke

Not less true is it that he who feels that God has given him a particular work to do can be happy only when earnestly engaged in its performance. Happy the youth who finds the place which his dreams have pictured. If he does not fill that place, he will not fill any to the satisfaction of himself or others. Nature never lets a man rest until he has found his place. She haunts him and drives him until all his faculties give their consent and he falls into his proper niche. A parent might just as well decide that the magnetic needle will point to Venus or Jupiter without trying it, as to decide what profession his son shall adopt.

              —O. S. Marden, from
              Pushing to the Front

When I hear a young man spoken of as giving promise of high genius, the first question I ask about him is always, does he work.

              —John Ruskin

Things don't turn up in this world until somebody turns them up.

              —James A. Garfield

He who improves an opportunity sows a seed which will yield fruit in opportunity for himself and others. Every one who has labored honestly in the past has aided to place knowledge and comfort within the reach of a constantly increasing number.

              —O. S. Marden, from
              Pushing to the Front

EARTH VICTORY

How stubbornly I cleared the field
And pulverized the stony land
And I watered all its sterile sand
To make the barren acres yield.

But when I gained the victory
And moulded to my will the ground,
I rested from my work and found
The subtle earth had moulded me.

              —Lewis Morgan

GOD'S WORK

What we see here of this world is but an expression of God's will, so to speak—a beautiful earth and sky and sea—beautiful affections and sorrows, wonderful changes and developments of creation, suns rising, stars shining, birds singing, clouds and shadows changing and fading, people loving each other, smiling and crying, the multiplied phenomena of Nature, multiplied in fact and fancy, in Art and Science, in every way that a man's intellect or education or imagination can be brought to bear.—And who is to say that we are to ignore all this, or not value them and love them, because there is another unknown world yet to come? Why that unknown future world is but a manifestation of God Almighty's will, and a development of Nature, neither more or less than this in which we are, and an angel glorified or a sparrow on a gutter are equally parts of His creation. The light upon all the saints in Heaven is just as much and no more God's work, as the sun which shall shine tomorrow upon this infinitesimal speck of creation.

—*William Makepeace Thackeray*

The trouble with us is that we are ever looking for a princely chance of acquiring riches, or fame, or worth. We are dazzled by what Emerson calls the "shallow Americanism" of the day. We are expecting mastery without apprenticeship, knowledge without study, and riches by credit.

—*O. S. Marden, from*
Pushing to the Front

The crowning fortune of a man is to be born to some pursuit which finds him in employment and happiness, whether it be to make baskets, or broadswords, or canals, or statues, or songs.

—*Ralph Waldo Emerson*

Leisure is a beautiful garment but it will not do for constant wear.

—*Anonymous*

If there's a job to be done, I always ask the busiest man in my parish to take it on and it gets done.

—*Lyman Beecher*

Unless I liked my daily tasks
I'd feel a strong misgiving
That though I did my work to live
I wasn't really living.

—*Rebecca McCann, from*
Cheerful Cherub

Employment is nature's physician, and is essential to human happiness.

—*Galen*

The man who never makes any mistakes never makes anything. Many chips, broken instruments, cuts and bruises, belong to the history of any beautiful statue. Persist in spite of everything.

—*Maltbie D. Babcock*

Work is my recreation,
The play of faculty; a delight like that
In darting through the water,—
Nothing more.

—*Henry Wadsworth Longfellow,
from "Michael Angelo"*

To work all day long just for money
Mid turmoil and hurry and strife
Might make me a pretty good living
But wouldn't make much of a life.

—*Rebecca McCann, from*
Cheerful Cherub

"Make me as good a hammer as you know how," said a carpenter to the blacksmith in a New York village before the first railroad was built; "Six of us have come to work on the new church, and I've left mine at home." "As good a one as I know how?" asked David Maydole, doubtfully, "but perhaps you don't want to pay for as good a one as I know how to make." "Yes, I do," said the carpenter, "I want a good hammer."

It was indeed a good hammer that he received, the best, probably, that had ever been made. By means of a longer hole than usual, David had wedged the handle in its place so that the head could not fly off, a wonderful improvement in the eyes of the carpenter, who boasted of his prize to his companions. They all came to the shop the next day, and each ordered such a hammer. When the contractor saw the tools, he ordered two for himself, asking that they be made a little better than the men. "I can't make any better ones," said Maydole, "when I make a thing I make it as well as I can, no matter whom it is for."

The storekeeper soon ordered two dozen, a supply unheard of in his previous business. A New York dealer in tools came to the village to sell his wares, and bought all the storekeeper had, and left a standing order for all the blacksmith could make. . . . They were usually sold without any warrant of excellence, the word "Maydole" stamped on the head being universally considered a guaranty of the best article the world could produce.

—*O. S. Marden, from*
Pushing to the Front

Occupation is one great source of enjoyment. No man, properly occupied, was ever miserable.

—*L. E. Landon*

Life is hardly respectable if it has no generous task, no duties or affections that constitute a necessity of existing. Every man's task is his life-preserver.

—*G. B. Emerson*

home

A good relationship has a pattern like a dance and is built on some of the same rules. . . . When each partner loves so completely that he has forgotten to ask himself whether or not he is loved in return; when he only knows that he loves and is moving to its music—then, and then only, are two people able to dance perfectly in tune to the same rhythm.

—Anne Morrow Lindbergh, from Gift from the Sea

The mother's yearning, that completest type of life within another life which is the essence of human love, feels the presence of the cherished child, even in the base degraded man.

—George Eliot

MOTHER

As years ago we carried to your knees
The tales and treasures of eventful days,
Knowing no deed too humble for your
    praise,
Nor any gift too trivial to please,
So still we bring, with older smiles and
    tears,
What gifts we may, to claim the old, dear
    right;
Your faith, beyond the silence and the
    night,
Your love still close and watching through
    the years.

—Kathleen Norris

It is indeed at home that every man must be known by those who would make a just estimate either of his virtue or felicity; for smiles and emboidery are alike occasional, and the mind is often dressed for show in painted honor and fictitious benevolence.

—Samuel Johnson

MEASURES

Things near us are seen of the size of life: Things at a distance are diminished to the size of understanding. We measure the universe by ourselves. . . .

I should like well enough to spend the whole of my life in traveling abroad, if I could anywhere borrow another life to spend afterwards at home!

—William Hazlitt

Unhappy is the man for whom his own mother has not made all other mothers venerable.

—Jean Paul Richter

When home is ruled according to God's Word, angels might be asked to stay with us, and they would not find themselves out of their element.

—Charles Haddon Spurgeon

MOTHERHOOD

Mother of Christ long slain, forth glided
she,
  Following the children joyously astir
Under the cedars and the olive-tree,
  Pausing to let their laughter float to her.
Each voice an echo of a voice more dear,
  She saw a little Christ in every face.
When lo! another woman, passing near,
  Yearned o'er the tender life that filled
    the place,
And Mary sought the woman's hand, and
    said:
  "I know thee not, yet know thee memory-
    tossed
And what hath led thee here, as I am led—
  These bring to thee a child beloved and
    lost."
    "How radiant was my little one!
      And He was fair,
    Yea fairer than the fairest sun,
    And like its rays through amber spun
      His sun-bright hair,
    Still, I can see it shine and shine!
      "Even so," the woman said, "was
        mine."

    "His ways were ever darling ways,"
      And Mary smiled,—
    "So soft and clinging! Glad relays
    Of love were all his precious days—
      My little child
    Was like an infinite that gleamed."
    "Even so was mine," the woman
      dreamed.

    Then whispered Mary: "Tell me, thou
      Of thine!" And she:
    "Oh, mine was rosy as a bough
    Blooming with roses, sent, somehow,
      To bloom for me!
    His balmy fingers left a thrill
    Within my breast that warms me still."

Then gazed she down some wilder, darker
    hour
And said, when Mary questioned knowing
    not:
"Who art thou, mother of so sweet a
    flower?"
"I am the mother of Iscariot."

—*Agnes Lee*

I want to give and take from my children
and husband, to share with friends and
community, to carry out my obligations to
man and to the world, as a woman, as an
artist, as a citizen.

But I want first of all—in fact, as an end
to these other desires—to be at peace with
myself. I want a singleness of eye, a purity
of intention, a central core to my life that
will enable me to carry out these obligations and activities as well as I can.

—*Anne Morrow Lindbergh, from*
Gift from the Sea

Any feeling that takes a man away from
his home is a traitor to the household.

—*Henry Ward Beecher*

He is happiest, be he king or peasant, who
finds peace in his home.

—*Goethe*

OF ANCIENT SHACKLES

I am among those unregenerates
Who do not seek "New Freedom," who
   enjoy
The ancient shackles of old-fashioned love,
Of faith and duty, and would not destroy
All moorings of the spirit that are old.
I like old-fashioned, peaceful firesides,
The steadfastness old homes and gardens
   knew;
I hold the old belief that love abides,
The old sustaining credences of men
That God must be the nurture of the soul,
That He will lean and listen to a prayer
And watches every man move toward his
   goal.
I am an unemancipated one
Who wears such fetters with a full content;
I see New Freedom's tortured restlessness
And of my bonds am deeply reverent.

—Adelaide Love

I know well those who marry with love and without money have sorry days but their nights shine with scarlet moons and the music of white sea-horses calling. Yet every moon is pressed by a time guide and the sea would be silly and inconceivable without a bottom. So love must have roots and time tries every troth.

Of a certainty love does teach eternity and is like a river that never dries up and has ever new water to succeed that which passeth. They who wear rings have an image of eternity on their fingers. They who handle a wheel have an emblem of eternity before them. For to what part soever of the ring or wheel one looks, one will still see another part beyond it.

—Carl Sandburg, from
Remembrance Rock

Educate your children to self-control, to the habit of holding passion and prejudice and evil tendencies subject to an upright and reasoning will, and you have done much to abolish misery from their future lives and crimes from society.

Knowledge does not comprise all which is contained in the large term of education. The feelings are to be disciplined; the passions are to be restrained; true and worthy motives are to be inspired; a profound religious feeling is to be instilled, and pure morality inculcated under all circumstances. All this is comprised in education.

—Daniel Webster

All that I have ever accomplished in life, I owe to my mother.

—Dwight L. Moody

All that I am or hope to be I owe to my angel mother.

—Abraham Lincoln

It is a wise father that knows his own child.

—William Shakespeare, from
Merchant of Venice

GOD HAS BEEN GOOD TO ME

I've a nice little place in the country
Where I hang my cares on a tree,
And my heart cries out, when I look
    about—
"God has been good to me!"

There's a loving face in the doorway
Where birds sing merrily,
And the children rush up with the family
    pup.
Yes, God has been good to me.

I might have been a millionaire,
With a mansion on the hill.
But I like things just the way they are,
And I guess I always will.

For I receive a million kisses—
I'm as rich as I can be!
And I always say, when I kneel to pray;
"God, You've been good to me."

—*Nick Kenny*

Without hearts there is no home.

—*Lord Byron*

THE LABORER

We have a bed, and a baby too,
My wife!
We have work besides, we have work for
    two,
And we have the sun, and the wind, and
    the rain,
And we only need one little thing more,
To be as free as the birds that soar:
Only time.

When we go through the fields on the Sun-
    day morn,
My child,
And far and away o'er the bending corn,
We see the swarming swallows flash,
Then we only need a bit of a dress,
To have the birds' bright loveliness:
Only time.

The storm is gathering black as jet,
Feel the poor.
Only a little eternity yet;
We need nothing else, my wife, my child,
Except all things through us that thrive,
To be bold as the birds through the air
    that drive:
Only time!

—*Richard Dehmal*

The child is father of the man.

—*William Wordsworth, from*
"My Heart Leaps Up When I Behold"

To the man who has had a mother, all
women are sacred for her sake.

—*Jean Paul Richter*

THIS DAY AND AGE

My lord and master is a one
Who's nearly always late,
But ever does he say a grace
Before his breakfast plate.

"Go with us, God, throughout this day,"
So does he supplicate:
 (But You will have to hurry, God,
He hasn't time to wait!)

—*Elizabeth Draper*

PLAIN ADVICE TO MARRIED PEOPLE

The writer here in much affection sends
This plain advice to his young married
friends;
Should you the friendly hints receive, they
may
Subserve your interest in a future day.
Your various duties learn—and always
move
By rule—and let your actions spring from
love.

1. Yourselves, your tempers to each other
   suit,
   And rather yield, than carry on dispute.
2. Be emulous of that exalted sense,
   Which fears to give and scorns to take
   offense.
3. Should small disputes arise, in patience
   wait;
   A little time may set the matter
   straight.
4. If one speaks rashly in an angry fit,
   The other must be deaf and silent sit.
5. Never lose sight of what the Scriptures
   say:
   The man should rule in love—the wife
   obey.
6. Let all dissentions in the closet end,
   And never bring them up before a
   friend.
7. Your mutual duties study when alone;
   And when with others, prove your
   hearts are one.
8. Your neighbors, visiting, will then per-
   ceive
   How different from the world believers
   live.
9. Careful attend God's worship every
   day,
   Nor suffer trifles to create delay.
10. Duties performed in proper time and
    place
    Add to religion a superior grace.
11. Consult each other always; often pray

What's best to do, and what to give
away.
12. Be firm and regular, whate'er it cost;
    Good works ill done will prove but
    labor's lost.
13. Be frugal, prudent, yet not meanly
    near,
    The Christian show in all you eat and
    wear.
14. At home, abroad, keep this in constant
    view
    Not what you may, but what you ought
    to do.

—Tyron Edwards, from
The Family Treasury

The first sure symptom of a mind in health,
is rest of heart, and pleasure felt at home.

—Edward Young

Let France have good mothers and she will
have good sons.

—Napoleon

TO MY MOTHER

I've gone about for years I find
With eyes half blind,
Squandering golden hours
In search of flow'rs
That do not grow, it seems,
Except in dreams;
But in my wanderings
From place to place
I've found more fair no face—
No eyes more true than thine,
Oh Mother mine.

—Edward Salisbury Field, from
"The Quest"

BEFORE IT IS TOO LATE

If you have a gray-haired mother
  In the old home far away,
Sit you down and write the letter
  You put off from day to day.
Don't wait until her weary steps
  Reach Heaven's pearly gate.
But show her that you think of her,
  Before it is too late.

If you have a tender message,
  Or a loving word to say,
Don't wait till you forget it,
  But whisper it to-day.
Who knows what bitter memories
  May haunt you if you wait?
So make your loved one happy
  Before it is too late.

The tender word unspoken,
  The letters never sent,
The long forgotten messages,
  The wealth of love unspent;
For these some hearts are breaking,
  For these some loved ones wait;
Show them that you care for them
  Before it is too late.

            —George Bancroft Griffith

To make your children capable of honesty is the beginning of education.

            —John Ruskin

If I might control the literature of the household, I would guarantee the well being of the church and state.

            —Bacon

WHEN I COME HOME

When I come home, worn with the fretful
    day,
  And find you waiting with your smile
    of love,
  Your arms' soft pressure all my cares re-
    move,
Your lips' strange magic all my fears allay.

When I come home—when my feet seek
    the shrine
  Our love has builded for our worship
    sweet,
  I pass from out a world of sham and
    cheat
Into a tiny world of truth divine.

When I come home—it matters not how
    strong
  The battle has beset me—in that hour
  When I come home I feel your subtle
    power
Which flows in soothing waves, like a low
    song.

When I come home my wonder wakes
    afresh
  Before the mystery of your woman's
    way;
  The skill to take and keep my heart
    alway,
A captive thrilling in a magic mesh.

            —Edwin Carlile Litsey

As our families, so is society. If well ordered, well instructed, and well governed, they are the springs from which go forth the streams of national greatness and prosperity—of civil order and public happiness.

            —W. M. Thayer

assurance

JESUS AND I

I can not do it alone;
  The waves run fast and high,
And the fogs close chill around,
  And the light goes out in the sky;
But I know we two shall win in the end—
  Jesus and I.

I can not row it myself,
  My boat on the raging sea;
But beside me sits Another,
  Who pulls or steers with me;
And I know that we too shall come into
    port—
  His child and He.

Coward and wayward and weak,
  I change with the changing sky,
To-day so eager and brave,
  To-morrow not caring to try;
But He never gives in, so we two shall
    win—
  Jesus and I.

—*Dan Crawford*

THOU ART COMING TO A KING

Thou art coming to a King,
Large petitions with thee bring
For His grace and power are such
None can ever ask too much.

—*John Newton*

We must get rid of fear; we cannot act at all till then. A man's acts are slavish, not true but specious; his very thoughts are false, he thinks too as a slave and coward, till he has got fear under his feet.

—*Thomas Carlyle*

Christ's death was not simply the world's example; it was the world's sacrifice. He died not merely as a martyr to the truth. His death is the world's life!

—*F. W. Robertson*

GOOD INTENTIONS

Many a good intention dies from inattention. If, through carelessness or indolence, or selfishness a good intention is not put into effect, we have lost an opportunity, demoralized ourselves, and stolen from the pile of possible good. To be born and not fed, is to perish. To launch a ship and neglect it is to lose it. To have a talent and bury it, is to be a "wicked and slothful servant." For in the end we shall be judged, not alone by what we have done, but by what we could have done.

—*Maltbie D. Babcock*

I beg you take courage; the brave soul can mend even disaster.

—*Catherine of Russia*

Confidence is king; confidence performs the impossible. Doubt is destructive and kills our efforts. No man can do his best when his mind is filled with doubt.

—*O. S. Marden, from* Conquest of Worry

AT EVENTIDE

I want to know, when day is done,
That life has been worth living—
That I have brought somebody joy
Through kind, unselfish giving.

I want to feel, when evening falls,
And shadows quickly lengthen,
That I have made some body glad,
Some weakness I have strengthened.

I want to know, that come what may,
I've left some cheer and gladness;
I want to know, that on my way,
I've banished someone's sadness.

I want to feel, at close of day,
That someone's cares were lighter;
Because of kindness I have done,
May someone's life be brighter.

—*Raymond Orner*

The league between virtue and nature engages all things to assume a hostile front to vice. The beautiful laws and substances of the world persecute and whip the traitor. He finds that things are arranged for truth and benefit, but there is no den in the wide world to hide a rogue. . . . Commit a crime, and the earth is made of glass.

—*Ralph Waldo Emerson, from* "Compensation"

We lend power to the things we fear!

—*O. S. Marden, from* Conquest of Worry

His joy is not that he has got the crown
But that the power to win the crown is his.

—*William Shakespeare*

Fear is born of ignorance. We fear, because we are not awake to our divine possibilities; we have discovered only a small part of our power, our resources; the vast reservoirs of strength and plenty that lie within us are unfathomed.

—*O. S. Marden, from* Conquest of Worry

WHIRRING WHEELS

Lord, when on my bed I lie,
Sleepless, unto Thee I'll cry;
When my brain works overmuch,
Stay the wheels with Thy soft touch.
Just a quiet thought of Thee,
And of Thy sweet charity,—
Just a little prayer, and then
I will turn to sleep again.

—*John Oxenham*

Self-confidence and self-respect give a sense of power which nothing else can bestow.

—*O. S. Marden, from* Pushing to the Front

We are always headed toward our fears, just as we are toward our hopes and our ambitions.

—*O. S. Marden, from* Conquest of Worry

GOD'S WORD

I paused last eve beside the blacksmith's
    door,
    And heard the anvil ring, the vesper's
        chime,
And looking in I saw upon the floor
    Old hammers, worn with beating years
        of time.
"How many anvils have you had?" said I,
    "To wear and batter all these hammers
        so?"
"Just one," he answered. Then with
    twinkling eye:
    "The anvil wears the hammers out, you
        know."
And so, I thought, the anvil of God's Word
    For ages skeptics' blows have beat upon,
Yet though the noise of falling blows was
    heard
    The anvil is unchanged; the hammers
       gone.

                  —*John Clifford*

What seems to us disagreeable egotism in others is often but a strong expression of confidence in their ability to attain. Great men have usually had great confidence in themselves. Wordsworth felt sure of his place in history, and never hesitated to say so. Dante predicted his own fame. . . . "Fear not," said Julius Caesar to his pilot frightened in a storm; "thou bearest Caesar and his good fortunes."

             —*O. S. Marden, from*
             Pushing to the Front

Fear is nothing more than a sense of being unable to cope with an expected crisis.

             —*O. S. Marden, from*
             Conquest of Worry

WITH WHOM IS NO VARIABLENESS, NEITHER SHADOW OF TURNING

It fortifies my soul to know
That, though I perish, Truth is so:
That, howsoe'er I strayed and range,
Whate'er I do, Thou dost not change.
I steadier step when I recall
That, if I slip, Thou dost not fall.

                      —*Clough*

We shall be glad—really glad—of everything that has come to us, no matter if it is sorrow or pain, when we find that our experience fits some one else's need—that some one else can build on our lives.

             —*Maltbie D. Babcock*

PSALM 121

I will lift up mine eyes unto the hills,
    from whence cometh my help.
My help cometh from the Lord,
    which made heaven and earth.
He will not suffer thy foot to be moved:
    he that keepeth thee will not slumber.
Behold, he that keepeth Israel
    shall neither slumber nor sleep.
The Lord is thy keeper:
    the Lord is thy shade
    upon thy right hand.
The sun shall not smite thee by day,
    nor the moon by night.
The Lord shall preserve thee from all evil:
    he shall preserve thy soul.
The Lord shall preserve
    thy going out and thy coming in
    from this time forth and even for
        evermore.

PSALM 23

The Lord is my shepherd; I shall not want.
　He maketh me to lie down in green pas-
　　tures:
he leadeth me beside the still waters.
　He restoreth my soul:
he leadeth me in the paths of righteousness
　for his name's sake.
Yea, though I walk through the valley of
　the shadow of death,
　I will fear no evil:
for thou art with me;
　thy rod and thy staff
　they comfort me.
Thou preparest a table before me
　in the presence of mine enemies:
thou anointest my head with oil;
　my cup runneth over.
Surely goodness and mercy shall follow me
　all the days of my life:
and I will dwell in the house of the Lord
　for ever.

The wise man endeavors to shine in himself; the fool to outshine others. The first
is humbled by the sense of his own infir-
mities, the last is lifted up by the discovery
of those which he observes in other men.
The wise man considers what he wants,
and the fool what he abounds in. The wise
man is happy when he gains his own appro-
bation, and the fool when he recommends
himself to the applause of those about him.

　　　　　　　　　　—*Joseph Addison*

God has put something noble and good into
every heart which his hand has created.

　　　　　　　　　　—*Mark Twain*

If God made no response except to perfect
faith, who could hope for help? He is the
God of sprouting seeds, and little vital beginnings.

　　　　　　　　　　—*Maltbie D. Babcock*

God's love is not rounded out until I re-
spond to it.

　　　　　　　　　　—*Maltbie D. Babcock*

God has promised to satisfy—but he did
not promise when. God has time enough,
and so have you. God has boundless resources, and his resources are yours. Can
you not trust him? Trust and wait. He
knows what is best for you, he has reasons
for denying you now, but in the end he
will satisfy.

　　　　　　　　　　—*Maltbie D. Babcock*

The deeper men go into life, the deeper
is their conviction that this life is not all.
It is an "unfinished symphony." A day
may round out an insect's life, and a bird
and a beast needs no tomorrow. Not so
with him who knows that he is related to
God and has felt "the power of an endless
life."

　　　　　　　　　　—*Maltbie D. Babcock*

success

WHAT IS SUCCESS?

He has achieved success who has lived well, laughed often, and loved much; who has gained the respect of intelligent men and the love of little children; who has filled his niche and accomplished his task; who has left the world better than when he found it, whether by an improved poppy, a perfect poem or a rescued soul; who has never lacked appreciation for earth's beauty or failed to express it; who has always looked for the best in others and given the best he had; whose life has ever been an inspiration; whose memory is a benediction.

—Mrs. A. J. Stanley

The successful men of to-day are men of one overmastering idea, one unwavering aim, men of single and intense purpose.

—O. S. Marden, from
Pushing to the Front

Ideas go booming through the world louder than cannon. Thoughts are mightier than armies. Principles have achieved more victories than horsemen or chariots.

—W. M. Paxton

It's not the things I failed to do
That makes me wipe this eye—
It's things I should and could have done
And simply failed to try.

—Rebecca McCann, from
Cheerful Cherub

Lives of great men all remind us
We can make our lives sublime,
And, departing, leave behind us
Footprints, on the sands of time;—

Footprints, that perhaps another
Sailing o'er life's solemn main,
A forlorn and shipwreck'd brother,
Seeing, shall take heart again.

—Henry Wadsworth Longfellow, from
"Psalm of Life"

Want of constancy is the cause of many a failure, making the millionaire of to-day a beggar to-morrow. Show me a really great triumph that is not the reward of persistence.

—O. S. Marden, from
Pushing to the Front

The talent of success is nothing more than doing what you can do well, and doing well whatever you do without a thought of fame. If it comes at all it will come because it is deserved, not because it is sought after.

—Henry Wadsworth Longfellow

Success is the child of two very plain parents—punctuality and accuracy.

—O. S. Marden, from
Pushing to the Front

Nor fame I slight, nor for her favors call:
She comes unlooked for, if she comes at all.

—*Alexander Pope, from
"Temple of Fame"*

A man may be festooned with the whole haberdashery of success, and go to his grave a castaway.

—*Rudyard Kipling*

The stoutest timber stands on Norwegian rocks, where tempests rage, and long, hard winters reign. The muscles are seen most fully developed in the brawny arm that plies the hammer. Even so, the most vigorous and healthy piety is that which is ever active in a busy world, which has difficulties to battle with, which has its hands full of good works, which has neither time nor room for evil, but, aiming at great things for God and man, promptly dismisses temptation with Nehemiah's answer: "I have a great work to do, therefore, I cannot come down."

—*Bishop McIlvain*

A man would do nothing, if he waited until he could do it so well that no one would find fault with what he has done.

—*John Henry Newman*

To character and success, two things, contradictory as they may seem, must go together—humble dependence and manly independence; humble dependence on God, and manly reliance on self.

—*William Wordsworth*

I want, by understanding myself, to understand others. I want to be all that I am capable of becoming. . . . This all sounds very strenuous and serious. But now that I have wrestled with it, it's no longer so. I feel happy—deep down. All is well.

—*Katherine Mansfield*

There are three things essential to success in life—conscientiousness, concentration, continuity. In extremity it is character that saves a man. To one object the lines of life should converge. This should be the focal-point of thought and feeling. We must not scatter our powers. Continuity is not incompatible with change; it is the reverse of a fragmentary and desultory mode of life. Every true life is a unit, an organic whole. There is advantage in continuity of place as well as purpose.

—*Asa Dodge Smith*

No one can pursue a worthy object steadily and persistently with all the powers of his mind, and yet make his life a failure.

—*O. S. Marden, from
Pushing to the Front*

PART IV
EVENING

EVENING

Evening. The heat lessened. Shadows lengthen pointing longer and longer toward Night. The day is ripened and a cool calmness comes. The workman's whistle is silent, the traffic is at leisure, the household gathers together its own, and the day is crowned with intimate charm. Stars light the sky.

Man met his test in the heat of Noon, or he didn't as the case might be. Now the sun that spotlighted him shows his deeds, silhouettes his influence. His achievements reward him. His failures cost him. Man reflects upon it all. He hoards the memories of Dawn, mirthful thoughts of Morning, and indelible awareness of Noon, and meets with himself in the Evening.

—May Detherage

Day, like a weary pilgrim, had reached the western gate of heaven, and Evening stooped down to unloose the latchets of his sandal shoon.

*—Henry Wadsworth Longfellow
from* Hyperion

EVENING

I know the night is near at hand.
  The mists lie low on hill and bay,
The autumn sheaves are dewless, dry;
  But I have had the day.

Yes, I have had, dear Lord, the day;
  When at Thy call I have the night,
Brief be the twilight as I pass
  From light to dark, from dark to light.

—S. Weir Mitchell

THERE IS NO WEALTH
BUT LIFE

That country is the richest which nourishes the greatest number of noble and happy human beings; that man is richest who, having perfected the functions of his own life to the utmost, has also the widest helpful influence, both personal, and by means of his possessions, over the lives of others.

—John Ruskin

integrity

Character must stand behind and back up everything—the sermon, the poem, the picture, the play. None of them is worth a straw without it.

—*Josiah Gilbert Holland*

GOD GIVE US MEN

God give us men! A time like this demands
  Strong minds, great hearts, true faith, and ready hands;
Men whom the lust of office does not kill;
  Men whom the spoils of office cannot buy;
Men who possess opinions and a will;
  Men who have honor; men who will not lie;
Men who can stand before a demagogue
  And damn his treacherous flatterings without winking;
Tall men, sun-crowned, who live above the fog
  In public duty and in private thinking!
For while the rabble, with their thumb-worn creeds,
Their large professions and their little deeds
Mingle in selfish strife, lo! Freedom weeps!
Wrong rules the land, and waiting Justice sleeps.

—*Josiah Gilbert Holland,*
  "The Day's Demand"

Accuracy is the twin brother of honesty: inaccuracy of dishonesty.

—*C. Simmons*

And during that long and fearful struggle, I do not remember one of his followers ever being convicted of a political offense, and during this period crimes of violence were very rare. There is not such record in our history. Neither in classic nor in modern times can the man be produced who held a million of people in his right hand so passive. It was due to the consistency and unity of a character that had hardly a flaw. I do not forget your soldiers, orators, or poets—any of your leaders. But I when I consider O'Connell's personal disinterestedness,—his rare, brave fidelity to every cause his principles covered, no matter how unpopular or how embarrassing to his main purpose, that clear far-reaching vision, true heart which, on most moral and political questions, set him so much ahead of his times;—I am ready to affirm that he was, all things considered, the greatest man the Irish race ever produced.

—*Wendell Phillips*

Be not hasty to cast off every aspersion that is cast on you. Let them alone for awhile, and then, like mud on your clothes, they will rub off of themselves.

—*Dr. Murray*

Character is power—is influence; it makes friends; creates funds; draws patronage and support; and opens a sure and easy way to wealth; honor, and happiness.

—*J. Hawes*

CHEATING

1. Cheating is underhand; it kills self-respect and destroys character.
2. Cheating is deception; it cultivates intentional dishonesty.
3. Cheating is fraudulence; it makes of a person a counterfeit.
4. Cheating is compromise; it is stooping to disgrace.
5. Cheating is lying; it falsely asserts an unpossessed knowledge.
6. Cheating is theft; it gets value falsely, without the price thereof.
7. Cheating is sin; it is a wilful violation of the will of God.

—Frank H. Leavell, from
Master's Minority

Character is power, and is the best advertisement in the world.

—O. S. Marden, from
Pushing to the Front

We cannot long deceive the world, for that other self, who ever stands in the shadow of ourselves holding the scales of justice, that telltale in the soul, rushes to the eye or into the manner and betrays us.

But manners, while they are the garb of the gentleman, do not constitute or finally determine his character. Mere politeness can never be a substitute for moral excellence, any more than the bark can take the place of the heart of the oak. It may well indicate the kind of wood below, but not always whether it be sound or decayed. Etiquette is but a substitute for good manners and is often but their mere counterfeit.

Sincerity is the highest quality of good manners.

The following recipe is recommended to those who wish to acquire genuine good manners:—

Of Unselfishness, three drachms;

Of the Tincture of Good Cheer, one ounce;

Of Essence of Heart's-Ease, three drachms;

Of the Extract of the Rose of Sharon, four ounces;

Of the Oil of Charity, three drachms, and no scruples;

Of the Infusion of Common Sense and Tact, one ounce;

Of the Spirit of Love, two ounces.

The Mixture to be taken whenever there is the slightest symptom of selfishness, exclusiveness, meanness, or I-am-better-than-you-ness.

—O. S. Marden, from
Pushing to the Front

Character is the diamond that scratches every other stone.

—Cyrus Augustine Bartol

THE GREATNESS OF A COUNTRY

Louis XIV asked Colbert how it was that, ruling so great and populous a country as France, he had been unable to conquer so small a country as Holland. "Because," said the minister, "the greatness of a country does not depend upon the extent of its territory, but on the character of its people."

—O. S. Marden, from
Pushing to the Front

understanding

TRUE READING

In this mood—and it is a mood which no thoughtful man can hope or ought to wish to escape—reading becomes less and less a searching for instructive and impressive facts, and more and more a quest after wisdom and truth and emotion. . . .

And thus reading becomes a patient tracing out of human emotion, human feeling, when confronted with the sorrows, the hopes, the motives, the sufferings which beckon us and threaten us on every side. . . .

In this mood the words of the wise fall like the tolling of sweet, grave bells upon the soul, the dreams of poets come like music heard at evening from the depths of some enchanted forest, wafted over a wide water; we know not what instrument it is whence the music wells, by what fingers swept, by what lips blown; but we know that there is some presence there that is sorrowful or glad, who has power to translate his dream into the concord of sweet sounds. Such a mood need not withdraw us from life, from toil, from kindly relationships, from deep affections; but it will rather send us back to life with a renewed joyful zest, with a desire to discern the true quality of beautiful things, of fair thoughts, of courageous hopes, of wise designs. It will make us tolerant, and forgiving, patient with stubbornness and prejudice, simple in conduct, sincere in word, gentle in deed; with pity for weakness, with affection for the lonely and the desolate, with admiration for all that is noble and serene and strong. . . .

A mind thus stored may have little grasp of facts, little garniture of paradox and jest; but it will be full of compassion and hope, of gentleness and joy.

—*Arthur Christopher Benson*

ENOUGH NOT ONE

The poor have little,
Beggars none;
The rich too much,
Enough not one.

—*Benjamin Franklin*

THE LESSON

My cot was down by the cypress grove,
And I sat by my window the whole night long,
And heard well up from the deep dark wood
A mocking-bird's passionate song.

And I thought of myself so sad and lone,
And my life's cold winter that knew no spring;
Of my mind so weary and sick and wild,
Of my heart too sad to sing.

But e'en I listened the mock-bird's song,
A thought stole into my saddened heart,
And I said, "I can cheer some other soul
By a carol's simple art."

For oft from the darkness of hearts and lives
Come songs that brim with joy and light,
As out of the gloom of the cypress grove
The mocking-bird sings at night.

So I sang a lay for a brother's ear
In a strain to soothe his bleeding heart,
And he smiled at the sound of my voice and lyre,
Though mine was a feeble art.

But at his smile I smiled in turn,
And into my soul there came a ray:
In trying to soothe another's woes
My own had passed away.

—*Paul Laurence Dunbar*

The truer we become, the more unerringly we know the ring of truth.

—*F. W. Robertson*

We ask for understanding,
But often what we mean
Is that all our friends will see us
As we'd rather we'd be seen.

—*Rebecca McCann, from*
Cheerful Cherub

LAUGHTER

In good truth, we know what a man is like by the things he finds laughable, we gauge both his understanding and his culture by his sense of the becoming and the absurd. If the capacity for laughter be one of the things which separates men from brutes, the quality of laughter draws a sharp dividing line between the trained intelligence and the vacant mind.

—*Agnes Repplier*

It is a common fault never to be satisfied with our fortune, nor dissatisfied with our understanding.

—*Frances Rochefoucauld*

A good life is the best way to understand wisdom and religion; because, by the experience and relishes of religion there is conveyed a sweetness to which all wicked men are strangers. There is, in the things of God, to those who practice them, a deliciousness that makes us love them, and that love admits us into God's cabinet, and strangely clarifies the understanding by the purification of the heart.

—*Jeremy Taylor*

Wisdom is the principal thing; therefore get wisdom: and with all thy getting get understanding.

—*Proverbs 4:7*

VAGRANT

He came to our threshold,
  A beggar unfed,
To plead for some water,
  A crust of bread.

He stammered a moment,
  Uncertain, afraid,
Expecting the common
  Refusal to aid.

I'd meant to deny him,
  As we sheltered do,
But my conscience reproached me,
  And he knew—he knew.

—*Henry Loukusa*

144

solitude

REFUGE

When stars ride in on the wings of dusk,
  Out on the silent plain,
After the fevered fret of day,
  I find my strength again.

Under the million friendly eyes
  That smile in the lonely night,
Close to the rolling prairie's heart,
  I find my heart for the fight.

Out where the cool long winds blow free,
  I fling myself on the sod;
And there in the tranquil solitude
  I find my soul—and God.

—*Lew Sarett*

SOLITUDE

For it is not physical solitude that actually separates one from other men, not physical isolation, but spiritual isolation. It is not the desert island nor the stony wilderness that cuts you from the people you love. It is the wilderness in the mind, the desert wastes in the heart through which one wanders lost and a stranger. When one is a stranger to oneself then one is estranged from others too. . . . Only when one is connected to one's own core is one connected to others.

—*Anne Morrow Lindbergh, from*
Gift from the Sea

GOD WITH US

Suffering is a very solitary thing. Great suffering brings upon the heart a sense of intense loneliness, and it needs all that God Himself can be to the stricken one. It might seem almost impossible that anything more than the peace of God could be promised, but there is a fuller promise yet. "The God of Peace shall be with you." Here language is exhausted. The portion of every praying one is "the peace of God" and when even that is not enough, "the God of Peace," Himself Emmanuel, stands besides you.

—*Pennyfather*

For solitude, however some may rave,
Seeming a sanctuary, proves a grave—
A sepulchre in which the living lie,
Where all good qualities grow sick and die.
I praise the Frenchman, his remark was
  shrewd—
"How sweet, how passing sweet, is solitude!
But grant me still a friend in my retreat,
Whom I may whisper, Solitude is sweet."

—*William Cowper*, "Retirement"

Solitude shows us what we should be;
Society shows us what we are.

—*Richard Cecil*

One hour of thoughtful solitude may nerve the heart for days of conflict—girding up its armor to meet the most insidious foe.

—*J. G. Percival*

Until I truly loved I was alone.

—*Mrs. C. S. S. Norton*

Solitude is of many kinds. There is the solitude of our own chamber—the solitude of the gentle walk—of the great library—of the gay ball room—of the desert. Solitude must not be confounded with retirement. A man may be solitary without retiring from the world; may seek retirement and yet not be solitary. Some are impatient of the human voice, others of the human countenance; the former are contemplative, the latter misanthropical. The former in their lonely walks would courteously return, rather pleased than pained, the silent salutation of the unobtrusive peasant; to the others, nature undeformed by the footsteps of man alone is tolerable.

One thing is certain, that those who can in truth affirm that they "never less alone than when alone," might generally add, that they never feel more lonely than when not alone.

—*Arthur Helps*

Conversation enriches the understanding, but solitude is the school of genius.

—*Edward Gibbons*

Solitude is a good school, but the world is the best theatre; the institution is best there, but the practice here; the wilderness hath advantage of discipline, and society opportunities of perfection.

—*Jeremy Taylor*

By all means, use sometimes to be alone;
Salute thyself; see what thy soul doth wear;
Dare to look in thy chest; for 'tis thine own,
And tumble up and down what thou findest there.

—*George Herbert*

He who could not sit
And sing contented in a desert isle,
His audience the mute trees and wandering winds,
His joy the grace and beauty of his song,
Should never lift his voice 'mong mortal men.

—*Alexander Smith*

At times you ought to stay alone
I make so bold as to advise
And just be friendly with your soul—
Your soul will miss you otherwise.

—*Rebecca McCann, from*
Cheerful Cherub

Solitude bears the same relation to the mind that sleep does the body. It affords it the necessary opportunities for repose and recovery.

—*W. G. Simms*

joy

GOD GIVE ME JOY

God give me joy in the common things:
In the dawn that lures, the eve that sings.

In the new grass sparkling after rain,
In the late wind's wild and weird refrain;

In the springtime's spacious field of gold,
In the precious light by winter doled.

God give me joy in the love of friends,
In their dear home talk as summer ends;

In the songs of children, unrestrained;
In the sober wisdom age has gained.

God give me joy in the tasks that press,
In the memories that burn and bless;

In the thought that life has love to spend,
In the faith that God's at journey's end.

God give me hope for each day that springs,
God give me joy in the common things!

—Thomas Curtis Clark

Joys are our wings, sorrows our spurs.

—Jean Paul Richter

Joy comes only as a dividend,
It cannot be purchased outright nor ac-
    cumulated through hoarded savings.
As I give my life unreservedly into the
    hands of God, He in turn reinvests it
    upon earth, spending freely where there
    is need.
Thus life—my only wealth—earns con-
    tinuous dividends of spiritual joy,
And there is the certain knowledge that the
    investment itself is secure.

—Carolyn Rhea, from
Such Is My Confidence

Some of you say, "Joy is greater than
sorrow," and others say, "Nay, sorrow is
the greater."

But I say unto you, they are inseparable.
Together they come, and when one sits
alone with you at your board, remember
that the other is asleep upon your bed.

Verily you are suspended like scales between your sorrow and your joy.

Only when you are empty are you at
standstill and balanced.

When the treasurer-keeper lifts you to
weigh his gold and his silver, needs must
your joy or your sorrow rise or fall.

—Kahlil Gibran, from The Prophet

O God, thou art my God; early will I seek
thee: my soul thirsteth for thee, my flesh
longeth for thee in a dry and thirsty land,
where no water is; To see thy power and
thy glory, so as I have seen thee in the
sanctuary. Because thy lovingkindness is
better than life, my lips shall praise thee.
Thus will I bless thee while I live: I will
life up my hands in thy name.

—Psalm 63:1-4

I will not cling to joys when Fate
Demands that I forsake them—
Life always brings new gifts to those
Whose hands are free to take them.

—Rebecca McCann, from
Cheerful Cherub

JOY IN ALL THINGS

"Joy" is a larger word than "happiness" or "amusement" or "diversion." It includes all of these, but much else,—trials, tests and tasks. Happiness is a thing of happenings. Amusement is turning aside to muse, or cultivating the Muses after work. Diversion is being put on another track for a little while. But joy belongs to all that happens, and to work as well as to amusement or diversion. . . .

It suffers and endures for that which is to be when the work is done, when the iron becomes steel, and rough marble a thing of beauty. In temptation, it finds the warrior's delight; in victory and defeat, if an honorable one, the comfort of knowing that God understands every campaign; if dishonorable one, the sad but hopeful joy of honest repentance and a new determination.

—*Maltbie D. Babcock*

The Lord is my strength and my shield; my heart trusted in him, and I am helped: therefore my heart greatly rejoiceth; and with my song will I praise him.

The Lord is their strength, and he is the saving strength of his anointed.

—*Psalm 28:7, 8*

True joy is a serene and sober motion; and they are miserably out that take laughter for rejoicing; the seat of it is within, and there is no cheerfulness like the resolution of a brave mind that has fortune under its feet.

—*Seneca*

He shall call upon me, and I will answer him:
I will be with him in trouble; I will deliver him, and honor him.

With long life will I satisfy him, and shew him my salvation.

—*Psalm 91:15, 16*

He walked by faith and not by sight,
By love and not by law;
The presence of the wrong or right
He rather felt than saw.

—*John Greenleaf Whittier*

Joy is more divine than sorrow, for joy is bread and sorrow is medicine.

—*Henry Ward Beecher*

We can do nothing well without joy, and a good conscience which is the ground of joy.

—*Richard Sibbes*

He who can conceal his joys is greater than he who can hide his griefs.

—*J. C. Lavater*

maturity

OUT IN THE FIELDS WITH GOD

The little cares that fretted me,
    I lost them yesterday,
Among the fields above the sea,
    Among the winds at play,
Among the lowing of the herds,
    The rustling of the trees,
Among the singing of the birds,
    The humming of the bees.

The foolish fears of what might pass
    I cast them all away
Among the clover-scented grass
    Among the new-mown hay,
Among the rustling of the corn
    Where drowsy poppies nod,
Where ill thoughts die and good are born—
    Out in the fields with God!

    —*Elizabeth Barrett Browning*

Perhaps middle age is, or should be, a period of shedding shells; the shell of ambition, the shell of material accumulations and possessions, the shell of the ego. Perhaps one can shed at this stage in life as one sheds in beach-living; one's pride, one's false ambitions, one's mask, one's armor. Was that armor not put on to protect one from the competitive world? If one ceases to compete, does one need it? Perhaps one can at last in middle age, if not earlier, be completely oneself. And what a liberation that would be! . . .

Woman must come of age by herself. This is the essence of "coming of age"— to learn how to stand alone.

    —*Anne Morrow Lindbergh, from*
    Gift from the Sea

I know a smiling old lady, who says she has made it a life habit to expect, every morning when she awakes, to have a glorious day. She says she looks toward the coming day as she would toward a journey she was taking, and she is always expecting some new delight, some wonderful experience. She says that the very thought that the day holds beautiful things in store for those who expect them, for those who believe they are coming to them, has been a constant inspiration. It has helped to bring her the very things she expects.

    —*O. S. Marden, from*
    Conquest of Worry

My foot standeth in an even place: in the congregations will I bless the Lord.

    —*Psalm 26:12*

Island-precepts, I might call them if I could define them, signposts toward another way of living. Simplicity of living, as much as possible, to retain a true awareness of life. Balance of physical, intellectual, and spiritual life. Work without pressure. Space for significance and beauty. Time for solitude and sharing. Closeness to nature to strengthen understanding and faith in the intermittency of life. life of the spirit, creative life, and the life of human relationships.

    —*Anne Morrow Lindbergh, from*
    Gift from the Sea

To see the golden sun, the azure sky, the outstretched ocean; to walk upon the green earth, and be lord of a thousand creatures; to look down yawning precipices or over distant sunny vales; to see the world spread out under one's feet on a map; to bring the stars near; to view the smallest insects through a microscope; to read history and consider the revolutions of empire and the successions of generations; to hear of the glory of Tyre, of Sidon, of Babylon, and of Susa, and to say all these were before me and are now nothing; to say I exist in such a point of time, and in such a point of space; to be a spectator and a part of its every-moving scene; to witness the change of seasons, of spring and autumn, of winter and summer; to feel hot and cold, pleasure and pain, beauty and deformity, right and wrong; to be sensible to the accidents of Nature; to consider the mighty world of eye and ear; to listen to the stock-dove's notes amid the forest deep; to journey over moor and mountain; to hear the midnight sainted choir; to visit lighted halls, or the cathedral's gloom, or sit in crowded theatres and see life itself mocked; to study the works of art and refine the sense of beauty to agony; to worship fame, and to dream of immortality; to look upon the Vatican, and to read Shakespeare; to gather up wisdom of the ancients, and to pry into the future; to listen to the trumpet of war, the shout of victory, to question history as to movements of the human heart; to seek for truth; to plead the cause of humanity; to overlook the world as if time and nature poured their treasures at our feet—to be and to do all this, and then in a moment to be nothing—to have snatched from us as a juggler's trick, or a phantasmagoria! . . .

It is thus, that, while we find our personal and substantial identity vanishing from us, we strive to gain a reflected and vicarious one in our thoughts: we do not like to perish wholly, and wish to bequeath our names at least, to posterity.

—*William Hazlitt*

AT EVENING

When sunset turns the lake to gold, beneath
    the sky's warm blue,
My eyes can almost look on God, so near
    His presence steals;
I feel a sudden tender thrill—the same a
    dreamer feels,
Who wakes from some vague reverie to see
    his dream come true.

I find God's smile in every tree, I know
    His kind eyes shine
When clouds are parted in the West; the
    misty, scented air
Is like a voice that to me and lifts my soul
    in prayer—
And—almost—as twilight grows, I feel His
    hand in mine.

—*Margaret E. Sangster, Jr.*

The shaping our own life is our own work. It is a thing of beauty, it is a thing of shame, as we ourselves make it. We lay the corner and add joint to joint, we give the proportion, we set the finish. It may be a thing of beauty and of joy forever. God forgive us if we pervert our life from putting on its appointed glory!

—*Ware*

We know enough now to begin to liberate man. Let us make the attempt upon ourselves; aided by religion, let us engrave upon our hearts the commandments of a new morality:

Thou shalt not be afraid of thy hidden impulses.

Thou shalt learn to respect thyself and then thou wilt love thy neighbor as thyself.

Thou shalt transcend inner anxiety, recognizing thy true competence and courage.

Thou shalt stand undismayed in the presence of grief. Thou shalt not deny the sadness of thy heart. Thou shalt make no detour around sorrow, but shall live through it, and by the aid of human togetherness and comradely sympathy thou shalt win dominion over sorrow.

Thou shalt eternally respect truth and tell it with kindness and also with firmness to all of thy associates, to the young child as well as to thy brother, and through truth shalt thou find healing and salvation.

Thou shalt search thy heart for the traces of immaturity and the temptations of childishness. Thou shalt reject all flight from freedom, all escape from maturity, as unworthy of thy person. Thou shalt turn away from all supine reliance upon authority, all solacing slavery to an omnipotent social father. Thou shalt seek together with thy brothers a kingdom of mature equality.

Thou shalt uproot from thy heart the false doubts and childish petulance which keep thee far from God. Thou shalt not make Him the scapegoat for thy emotional wounds and thy psychic scars. Thou shalt free thyself of the distortions which block

thy way to His presence, and by that freedom thou shalt commune at last with Him, the source of truth, the giver of peace.

—*Joshua Loth Liebman, from*
Peace of Mind

Like a morning dream, life becomes more and more bright the longer we live, and the reason of everything appears more clear. What has puzzled us before seems less mysterious, and the crooked paths look straighter as we approach the end.

—*Henry Richter*

The gem cannot be polished without friction, nor a man be perfected without trials.

—*Chinese Proverb*

The measure of the master is his success in bringing all men round to his opinion twenty years later.

—*Ralph Waldo Emerson*

When a noble life has prepared for old age, it is not decline that it reveals, but the first days of immortality.

—*Madame de Stael*

THE FLIGHT OF YOUTH

There are gains for all our losses,
  There are balms for all our pain:
But when youth, the dream, departs,
It takes something from our hearts,
  And it never comes again.

We are stronger, and are better,
  Under manhood's sterner reign:
Still we feel that something sweet
Followed youth, with flying feet,
  And will never come again.

Something beautiful is vanished,
  And we sigh for it in vain:
We behold it everywhere,
On the earth, and in the air,
  But it never comes again.

—*R. H. Stoddard*

They are poor
That have lost nothing; they are poorer far
Who losing, have forgotten; they most poor
Of all who lose and wish they might forget.

—*Jean Ingelow*

Be noble! and the nobleness that lies
In other men, sleeping, but never dead,
Will rise in majesty to meet thine own.

—*James Russell Lowell*

Doubt is the accusing attorney in the Court
of Truth.

—*Anonymous*

WHAT IS GOOD

"What is the real good?"
I asked in musing mood.

Order, said the law court;
Knowledge, said the school;
Truth, said the wise man;
Love, said a maiden;
Beauty, said the page;
Freedom, said the dreamer;
Home, said the sage;
Fame, said the soldier;
Equity, the seer;

Then within my bosom
Softly this I heard:
"Each heart holds the secret;
Kindness is the word."

—*John Boyle O'Reilly*

Integrity without knowledge is weak and
useless.

In all things preserve integrity; and the
consciousness of thine own uprightness will
alleviate the toil of business, soften the
hardness of ill-success and disappointments
and give thee an humble confidence before
God, when the ingratitude of man, or the
iniquity of the times may rob thee of other
rewards.

—*William Paley*

The tendency of old age to the body, say
the physiologists, is to form bone. It is as
rare as it is pleasant to meet with an old
man whose opinions are not ossified.

—*J. F. Boyse*

patriotism

THE GETTYSBURG ADDRESS

Fourscore and seven years ago our fathers brought forth on this continent a new nation, conceived in liberty and dedicated to the proposition that all men are created equal.

Now we are engaged in a great civil war, testing whether that nation or any nation so conceived and so dedicated can long endure. We are met on a great battlefield of that war. We have come to dedicate a portion of that field as a final resting-place for those who here gave their lives that that nation might live. It is altogether fitting and proper that we should do this.

But, in a larger sense, we cannot dedicate, we cannot consecrate, we cannot hallow this ground. The brave men, living and dead, who struggled here have consecrated it far above our poor power to add or detract. The world will little note nor long remember what we say here, but it can never forget what they did here. It is for us the living, rather, to be dedicated here to the unfinished work which they who fought here have thus far so nobly advanced. It is rather for us to be here dedicated to the great task remaining before us—that from these honored dead we take increased devotion to that cause for which they gave the last full measure of devotion—that we here highly resolve that these dead shall not have died in vain, that this nation, under God, shall have a new birth of freedom, and that government of the people, by the people, for the people, shall not perish from the earth.

—*Abraham Lincoln*

Patriotism is not enough. I must have no hatred or bitterness towards anyone.

—*Edith Cavell*

When we say a patriot is one who loves his country, what kind of love is it we mean? . . . You have heard that the shroud has no pockets and the dead to whatever place they go carry nothing with them—you have heard that and you know its meaning is plain. . . . You have also heard the dead hold in their clenched hands only that which they have given away. In this we begin to approach the meaning of a patriot though we do not unlock the secret that hides in the bosom of a patriot. The dead hold in their clenched hands only that which they have given away. When men forget what is at the heart of that sentiment—and it is terribly sentimental—they are in danger of power being taken over by swine, or beasts of prey or men hollow with echoes and vanities. It has happened and the records and annals cry and moan with specific instances.

—*Carl Sandburg, from* Remembrance Rock

Sail on, O Ship of State!
Sail on, O Union, strong and great!
Humanity with all its fears,
With all the hopes of future years,
Is hanging breathless on thy fate!

—*Henry Wadsworth Longfellow, from* "The Building of the Ship"

I pledge you, I pledge myself, to a new deal for the American people.

—*Franklin Delano Roosevelt*

I HEAR AMERICA SINGING

I hear America singing, the varied carols I
hear:
Those of mechanics—each one singing his,
as it should be, blithe and strong;
The carpenter singing his, as he measures
his plank or beam;
The mason singing his, as he makes ready
for work, or leaves off work;
The boatman singing what belongs to him
in his boat—the deckhand singing on the
steamboat deck;
The shoemaker singing as he sits on his
bench—the hatter singing as he stands;
The wood-cutter's song—the ploughboy's
on his way in the morning, or at noon
intermission, or at sundown;
The delicious singing of the mother—or
of the young wife at work—or of the girl
sewing or washing—
Each singing what belongs to him or her
and to none else;
The day what belongs to the day—at night,
the party of young fellows, robust, friendly,
Singing with open mouths their strong
melodious songs.

—*Walt Whitman*

When it shall be said in any country in the
world, "My poor are happy, neither ignorance nor distress is to be found among
them; my jails are empty of prisoners, my
streets of beggars; the aged are not in want,
the taxes are not oppressive; the rational
world is my friend; because I am a friend
of its happiness." When these things can be
said, then can that country boast of its
constitution and its government.

—*Dean C. Dutton, from*
Quests and Conquests

If when I die I am still a dictator I will
certainly go down into the oblivion of all
dictators. If on the other hand I succeed in
establishing a truly stable foundation for a
democratic government, I will live forever
in every home in China.

—*Chiang Kai-shek*

This is the Voice of Freedom, General Mac-
Arthur speaking. People of the Philippines:
I have returned.

—*Douglas MacArthur*

Man's capacity for justice makes democracy
possible, but man's inclination to injustice
makes democracy necessary.

—*Reinhold Niebuhr*

'Tis not the babbling of an idle world,
Where praise and censure are at random
hurled,
That can the meanest of my thoughts con-
trol,
Or shake the settled purpose of my soul.
Free and large might their wild curses
roam,
If all, if all, alas! were well at home.

—*Charles Churchill, from*
"The Conference"

WHAT MAKES A NATION GREAT?

Not serried ranks with flags unfurled,
Not armored ships that gird the world,
Not hoarded wealth nor busy mills,
Not cattle on a thousand hills,
Not sages wise, nor schools nor laws,
Not boasted deeds in freedom's cause—
All these may be, and yet the state
In eye of God be far from great.

That land is great which knows the Lord,
Whose sons are guided by His word;
Where justice rules 'twixt man and man,
Where love controls in art and plan;
Where, breathing in his native air,
Each soul finds joy in praise and prayer—
Thus may our country, good and great,
Be God's delight—man's best estate.

—*Alexander Blackburn*

In the future days, which we seek to make secure, we look forward to a world founded upon four essential human freedoms. The first is freedom of speech and expression—everywhere in the world. The second is freedom of every person to worship God in his own way—everywhere in the world. The third is freedom from want—everywhere in the world. The fourth is freedom from fear—anywhere in the world!

—*Franklin Delano Roosevelt*

Justice, sir, is the great interest of man on earth. It is the ligament which holds civilized beings and civilized nations together.

—*Daniel Webster*

It is a common heresy and its graves are to be found all over the earth. It is the heresy that says you can kill an idea by killing a man, defeat a principle by defeating a person, bury truth by burying its vehicle.

Man may burn his brother at the stake, but he cannot reduce truth to ashes; he may murder his fellow man with a shot in the back, but he does not murder justice; he may slay armies of men, but as it is written, "truth beareth off the victory."

—*Adlai E. Stevenson*

One flag, one land, one heart, one hand,
One Nation, evermore!

—*Oliver Wendell Holmes, from*
"Voyage of the Good Ship Union"

I have nothing to offer but blood, toil, tears, and sweat.

—*Winston Churchill*

Humility must always be the portion of any man who receives acclaim earned in the blood of his followers and the sacrifices of his friends.

—*Dwight D. Eisenhower*

A PATRIOT

"When we say a patriot is one who loves his country," ran the voice of Justice Windom, "what kind of love do we mean? A love we can throw on a scale and see how much it weighs? A love we can take apart to see how it ticks? A love where with a yardstick we record how long, high, wide, it is? Or is a patriot's love of country a thing invisible, a quality, a human shade and breath, beyond all reckoning and measurement? These are questions. They are old as the time of man. And the answers to them we know in part. For we know when a nation goes down and never comes back, when a society or a civilization perishes, one condition may always be found. They forgot where they came from. They lost sight of what brought them along. The hard beginnings were forgotten and the struggles farther along. They became satisfied with themselves. Unity and common understanding there had been, enough to overcome rot and dissolution, enough to break through their obstacles. But the mockers came. And the deniers were heard. And vision and hope faded. And the custom of greeting became 'What's the use?' And men whose forefathers would go anywhere, holding nothing impossible in the genius of man, joined the mockers and deniers. They forgot where they came from. They lost sight of what had brought them along."

—*Carl Sandburg, from*
Remembrance Rock

With malice toward none; with charity for all; with firmness in the right, as God gives us to see the right, let us strive on to finish the work we are in.

—*Abraham Lincoln*

And so my fellow Americans: Ask not what your country can do for you—ask what you can do for your country.

—*John Fitzgerald Kennedy*

AMERICA

My country, 'tis of thee,
Sweet land of liberty,
  Of thee I sing;
Land where my fathers died,
Land of the pilgrims' pride,
From every mountain side
  Let freedom ring.

My native country, thee,
Land of the noble free—
  Thy name I love;
I love thy rocks and rills,
Thy woods and templed hills:
My heart with rapture thrills
  Like that above.

Let music swell the breeze,
And ring from all the trees
  Sweet freedom's song;
Let mortal tongues awake,
Let all that breathe partake,
Let rocks their silence break—
  The sound prolong.

Our fathers' God, to Thee,
Author of liberty,
  To Thee we sing;
Long may our land be bright
With freedom's holy light;
Protect us by Thy might
  Great God, our King.

—*Samuel Francis Smith*

INNOMINATUS

Breathes there the man with soul so dead,
Who never to himself hath said,
   "This is my own, my native land!"
Whose heart hath ne'er within him burned
As home his footsteps he hath turned
   From wandering on a foreign strand?
If such there breathe, go, mark him well;
For him no Minstrel raptures swell;
High though his titles, proud his name,
Boundless his wealth as wish can claim;
Despite these titles, power, and pelf,
The wretch, concentred all in self,
Living, shall forfeit fair renown,
And, doubly dying, shall go down
To the vile dust from whence he sprung,
Unwept, unhonoured, and unsung.

   —*Walter Scott, from*
"The Lay of the Last Minstrel"

IN FLANDERS' FIELDS

In Flanders' fields, the poppies blow
Between the crosses, row on row,
That mark our place; and in the sky
The larks, still bravely singing, fly,
Scarce heard amid the guns below.

We are the dead. Short days ago
We lived, felt dawn, saw sunset glow,
Loved and were loved; and now we lie
   In Flanders' fields.

Take up our quarrel with the foe!
To you, from failing hands, we throw
The torch. Be yours to hold it high!
If ye break faith with us who die
We shall not sleep, though poppies grow
   In Flanders' fields.

   —*John McCrae*

ROBERT E. LEE'S FAREWELL TO HIS ARMY

Headquarters, Army of Northern Virginia
April 10, 1865

After four years of arduous service, marked by unsurpassed courage and fortitude, the Army of Northern Virginia has been compelled to yield to overwhelming numbers and resources.

I need not tell the survivors of so many hard-fought battles, who have remained steadfast to the last, that I have consented to this result from no distrust of them; but, feeling that valor and devotion could accomplish nothing that could compensate for the loss that would have attended the continuation of the contest, I have determined to avoid the useless sacrifice of those whose past services have endeared them to their countrymen.

By the terms of the agreement, officers and men can return to their homes and remain until exchanged.

You may take with you the satisfaction that proceeds from the consciousness of duty faithfully performed, and I earnestly pray that a merciful God will extend to you His blessing and protection.

With an unceasing admiration of your constancy and devotion to your country, and a grateful remembrance of your kind and generous consideration of myself, I bid you all an affectionate farewell.

   —*R. E. Lee, General*

SALUTE TO OUR FLAG

I pledge allegiance to the flag of the United States of America and to the republic for which it stands; one nation under God, indivisible, with liberty and justice for all.

   —*Francis M. Bellamy*

PRAYER

O God our Father, history and experience have given us so many evidences of Thy guidance to nations and to individuals that we should not doubt Thy power or Thy willingness to direct us. Give us the faith to believe that when God wants us to do or not to do any particular thing, God finds a way of letting us know it.

May we not make it more difficult for Thee to guide us, but be willing to be led of Thee, that Thy will may be done in us and through us for the good of America and all mankind.

This we ask in Jesus' name. Amen.

—*Peter Marshall*

As long as there are sovereign nations possessing great power, war is inevitable.

—*Albert Einstein*

Off with your hat as the flag goes by!
  And let the heart have its say;
You're man enough for a tear in your eye
  That you will not wipe away.

—*Henry Curler Bunner,*
"The Old Flag"

He serves his party best who serves his country best.

—*Rutherford B. Hayes*

I tremble for my country when I reflect that God is just; that his justice cannot sleep forever; that considering numbers, nature, and natural means only, a revolution of the wheel of fortune, an exchange of situation, is among possible events; that it may become probable by supernatural interference! The Almighty has no attribute which can take sides with us in such a contest.

—*Thomas Jefferson, from*
Notes on Virginia

Every government degenerates when trusted to the rulers of the people alone. The people themselves therefore are its only safe depositories.

—*Thomas Jefferson*

If any one desires to know the leading and paramount object of my public life, the preservation of this Union will furnish him the key.

—*Henry Clay*

We have lived long, gentlemen, but this [Louisiana Purchase] is the noblest work of our lives.

—*Robert R. Livingston*

faith

MAN-TEST

When in the dim beginning of the years,
God mixed in man the raptures and the
    tears
And scattered through his brain the starry
    stuff,
He said, "Behold! yet this is not enough,
For I must test his spirit to make sure
That he can dare the Vision and endure.

"I will withdraw my Face,
Veil me in shadow for a certain space,
Leaving behind Me only a broken clue—
A crevice where the glory glimmers
    through,
Some whisper from the sky,
Some footprint in the road to track Me by.

"I will leave man to make the fateful guess,
Will leave him torn between the No and
    Yes,
Leave him unresting till he rests in Me,
Drawn upward by the choice that makes
    him free—
Leave him in tragic loneliness to choose,
With all in life to win or all to lose."

—Edwin Markham

PRAYER

Our Father, give us the faith to believe that
it is possible for us to live victoriously even
in the midst of dangerous opportunity that
we call crisis. Help us to see that there is
something better than patient endurance or
keeping a stiff upper lip, and that whistling
in the dark is not really bravery.

    Trusting in Thee, may we have the faith
that goes singing in the rain, knowing that
all things work together for good to them
that love Thee. Through Jesus Christ, our
Lord. Amen.

—Peter Marshall

Do not suppose, my dearest sons, that when
I have left you I shall be nowhere and no
one. Even when I was with you, you did
not see my soul, but knew that it was in
this body of mine from what I did. Believe
then that it is still the same, even though
you see it not.

—Cyrus the Great

Understanding is the reward of faith.
Therefore seek not to understand that thou
mayest believe, but believe that thou
mayest understand.

—Augustine

Faith affirms many things respecting which
the senses are silent, but nothing which
they deny. It is superior to their testi-
mony, but never opposed to it.

—Blaise Pascal

The dawn is not distant,
Nor is the night starless;
Love is eternal!
God is still God, and
His faith shall not fail us;
Christ is eternal!

*—Henry Wadsworth Longfellow, from
"Tales of a Wayside Inn"*

A RELIGION THAT DOES THINGS

Why is it that the very term "religious life" has come to voice the popular idea that religion is altogether divorced from ordinary life? That conception is the exact opposite of Christ's teachings. Faith, "reason grown courageous," as someone has called it, has become assurance to me now, not because the fight is easy and we are never worsted but because it has made life infinitely worth while, so that I want to get all I can out of it, every hour.

God help us not to neglect the use of a thing—like faith—because we do not know how it works! It would be a criminal offense in a doctor not to use the X ray even if he does not know how barium chloride makes Gamma rays visible. We must know that our opinions are not a matter of very great moment, except in so far as in what they lead us to do. I see no reason whatever to suppose that the Creator lays any stress on them either. Experience answers our problems—experience of faith and common sense. For faith and common sense, taken together, make reasonable service, which ends by giving us the light of life.

—*Sir Wilfred Grenfell*

Hope is a powerful creative force. I notice that people with great hope are usually successful, and that those with feeble expectations usually get what they expect.

O. S. Marden, from
Conquest of Worry

The just shall live by faith.

—*Romans 1:17*

BOUNDLESSNESS OF GOD'S PURPOSES

Let us beware of limiting God. Nothing is more foolish than to bound his purposes, especially in the matter of tuition, of the divine intention and discipline. What can iron ore in the furnace know of its fine and final uses, or a soul in affliction know of the "far-off interest of tears"? We have the minnow's rights, as Carlyle puts it, to say what we find in our little creek, but no right to bound the river and ocean beyond our small ideas. Let us ever be subject to hope in our life's tasks, saying, "It is the Lord," strengthening ourselves with a cheerful faith that His purpose is eternal, alive with love, overleaping the last limit of what we ask or think.

—*Maltbie D. Babcock*

Faith is the "white cane" for blind existence.
Beyond this single instant of life I am totally blind.
The maze ahead is obscured in darkness; each step holds potential terror.
But Faith goes before me to feel out the way that I might with confidence continue my journey.
Faith cannot see, but it can feel and conveys the message of having sensed the security of a safe surface upon which to tread.
Thus, with faith in my hand I need neither grope nor fear the terrors of darkness; for faith leads step by step along the path to God.

—*Carolyn Rhea, from*
Such Is My Confidence

Man's best powers point him Godward.

—*Charles H. Spurgeon*

If we want to be happy, we must hold the mental attitude which will produce happiness. If we want to be strong, we must refuse to harbor these forebodings, these pet superstitions, these haunting fears which weaken us. We must flood our minds with such a current of faith and courage and expectation, that there will not be room for the negative thoughts. We must march straight ahead secure in that faith which casteth out fear.

—O. S. Marden, from
Conquest of Worry

SUNWARD WITH GOD
We shall go sunward together,
   God and I,
And if some dark and cumulus cloud
   Should sweep the sky,
My heart shall turn sunward in singing;
   For I know
He will not ask my feet to walk
   Where He cannot go.

Oh, this is the faith triumphant!
   Whether I live or die,
We shall go sunward together,
   God and I.

—Sybil Armes

If there were no other argument for a future life, sin would furnish one never to be refuted; for it tells of a cause standing over between the Judge and ourselves, for the hearing and decision of which a time must certainly come.

—Isaac Taylor

"Should God be kind one day we shall have a Bible in our home and mayhap one or two other books. I will read to you and father what chapters and verses you wish. What a day that will be when we have two or three books in our house!"
The date was March, 1608. The place was England.

—Carl Sandburg, from
Remembrance Rock

As the marsh-hen secretly builds on the
   watery sod,
Behold I will build me a nest on the greatness of God:
I will fly in the greatness of God as the
   marsh-hen flies
In the freedom that fills all the space 'twixt
   the marsh and the skies:
By so many roots as the marsh-grass sends
   in the sod
I will heartily lay me a-hold on the greatness of God:
Oh, like to the greatness of God is the greatness within
The range of the marshes, the liberal
   marshes of Glynn.

—Sidney Lanier, from
"The Marshes of Glynn"

The greatest architect and the one most needed is hope.

—Lyman Beecher

A HYMN TO GOD THE FATHER

Wilt Thou forgive that sin where I begun,
  Which is my sin, though it were done
    before?
Wilt thou forgive that sin, through which
  I run,
  And do run still: though still I do de
    plore?
    When Thou hast done, Thou hast not
      done,
      For, I have more.

Wilt Thou forgive that sin by which I
  have won
  Others to sin? and made my sin their
    door?
Wilt thou forgive that sin which I did shun
  A year, or two: but wallowed in, a score?
    When Thou hast done, Thou hast not
      done,
      For, I have more.

I have a sin of fear, that when I have spun
  My last thread, I shall perish on the
    shore;
Swear by Thyself, that at my death Thy
  Son
  Shall shine as He shines now, and here-
    tofore;
    And, having done that, Thou hast
      done,
      I fear no more.

—John Donne

If faith produce no works, I see
That faith is not a living tree.
Thus faith and works together grow;
No separate life they e'er can know:
They're soul and body, hand and heart:
What God hath joined, let no man part.

    —Hannah More, from "Dan and Jane"

Christian faith is a grand cathedral,
with divinely pictured windows.—Standing without, you can see no glory, nor can
imagine any, but standing within every ray
of light reveals a harmony of unspeakable
splendors.

—Nathaniel Hawthorne

Christian, what of the night?
I cannot tell; I am blind.
I halt and hearken behind
If haply the hours will go back
And return to the dear dead light,
To the watchfires and stars that of old
Shone where the sky now is black,
Glowed where the earth now is cold.

    —A. C. Swinburne, from
    "A Watch in the Night"

Through the dark and stormy night
  Faith beholds a feeble light
  Up the blackness streaking;
Knowing God's own time is best,
In a patient hope I rest
  For the full day-breaking!

    —John Greenleaf Whittier, from
      "Barclay of Ury"

Whatever faith I have I pray it will be ever
a living and growing thing.

    —Carl Sandburg, from
      Remembrance Rock

resources

THERE IS NO FRIGATE LIKE A BOOK

There is no Frigate like a Book
To take us Lands away
Nor any Courses like a Page
Of prancing Poetry—
This Travel may the poorest take
Without offence of Toil—
How frugal is the Chariot
That bears the Human soul.

—*Emily Dickinson*

No life
Can be pure in its purpose and strong in its strife,
And all life not be purer and stronger thereby.

—*Owen Meredith, from "Lucile"*

When I consider what some books have done for the world, and what they are doing, how they keep up our hope, awaken new courage and faith, soothe pain, give an ideal life to those whose hours are cold and hard, bind together distant ages and foreign lands, create new worlds of beauty, bring down truth from heaven; I give eternal blessings for this gift, and thank God for books.

—*James Freeman Clarke*

The books I like the best are those
That give us more than what they say—
They simply open countless doors
Through which our thoughts can roam away.

—*Rebecca McCann, from*
Cheerful Cherub

One truth stands firm. All that happens in world history rests on something spiritual. If the spiritual is strong, it creates world history. If it is weak, it suffers world history.

—*Albert Schweitzer*

Good temper, like a sunny day, sheds a brightness over everything. It is the sweetener of toil and the soother of disquietude.

—*Washington Irving*

I am a part of all that I have met.

—*Alfred Tennyson, from "Ulysses"*

The art of being able to make good use of moderate abilities wins esteem, and often acquires more reputation than actual brilliancy.

—*Frances Rouchefoucauld*

Principles are very important, but they need to be adorned by the graces to render them attractive.

—*Anonymous*

THE BRIDGE BUILDER

An old man, going a lone highway,
Came at the evening, cold and gray,
To a chasm, vast and deep and wide,
Through which was flowing a sullen tide.
The old man crossed in the twilight dim;
The sullen stream had no fears for him;
But he turned when safe on the other side
And built a bridge to span the tide.

"Old man," said a fellow pilgrim near,
"You are wasting your strength with build-
    ing here;
Your journey will end with the ending
    day;
You never again must pass this way;
You have crossed the chasm, deep and
    wide—
Why build you the bridge at the eventide?"

The builder lifted his old gray head:
"Good friend, in the path I have come," he
    said,
"There followeth after me today
A youth whose feet must pass this way.
This chasm that has been naught to me,
To that fair-haired youth may a pitfall be.
He, too, must cross in the twilight dim;
Good friend, I am building the bridge for
    him."

—*Will Allen Dromgoole*

The best things are the nearest; the breath
in your nostrils, light in your eyes, flowers
at your feet, duties at your hand, the path
of God just before you.

Then do not grasp at the stars, but do
life's plain common work as it comes, certain that daily duties and daily bread are
sweetest things of life.

—*Anonymous*

The masterful mind is always positive.

—*O. S. Marden, from*
Conquest of Worry

An able man shows his spirit by gentle
words and resolute actions. He is neither
hot nor timid.

—*Phillip Dormer Chesterfield*

Books make up no small part of human
happiness.

—*Frederick the Great*

POSSESSIONS

The only test of possessions is use. The
talent that is buried is not owned. The
napkin and the hole in the ground are far
more truly the man's property, because
they are accomplishing something for him,
slothful and shameful though it be.

And what is a lost soul? Is it not one that
God cannot use, or one that cannot use
God? Trustless, prayerless, fruitless, love-
less—is it not so far lost? So may a man
have a soul that is lost and be dead while
he lives.

—*Maltbie D. Babcock*

Ability is a poor man's wealth.

—*M. Wren*

If I had but two loaves of bread, I would sell one and buy hyacinths, for they would feed my soul.

—*The Koran*

A SURPRISE

When Mr. Moffat, the missionary to Africa, on his return home for rest, met in a house in north of England an aged man, the Rev. Mr. Caldwell, to whom he was an entire stranger, Mr. Caldwell perceived that Mr. Moffat was a Scotchman, inquired the place of his birth, and was told, "Often away among the heathen, I think of my mother leading me, when a little boy to the Independence meeting at Falkirk, to hear an excellent minister named Caldwell."

As he spoke of his mother, old Mr. Caldwell rose up, with tears running down his cheeks and exclaimed, "Can it be? Are you little Robby Moffat? Is Moffat, the missionary, the boy his mother used to lead to my meeting house?" Till then the aged minister had not known that the little boy was the man who had done so much for Africa. O have faith in God.

—*Dean C. Dutton, from* Quests and Conquests

Love the beautiful,
Seek out the true,
Wish for the good,
And the best do.

—*Moses Mendelssohn*

It is a sad thing when a man has either a reputation beyond his merit, or an ambition beyond his ability.

—*S. Beatty*

Talent made a poor appearance until he married perseverance.

—*Anonymous*

LISTENING TO SCANDAL

No one loves to tell a tale of scandal but to him that loves to hear it. Learn, then, to rebuke and silence the distracting tongue, by refusing to hear. Never make your ear the grave of another's good name.

—*Tyron Edwards, from* The Family Treasury

It is told of David Hume, the great skeptic, that he once went to listen to the preaching of John Brown of Haddington. "That man is for me," Hume saïd, "he means what he says; he speaks as if Jesus Christ were at his elbow."

—*Arthur Helps*

All is but lip-wisdom which wants experi-perience.

—*Philip Sydney*

Only action gives to life its strength, as only moderation gives it its charm.

—*Jean Paul Richter*

Education is the cheap defense of nations.

—*Edmund Burke*

Sin has many tools but a lie is the handle which fits them all.

—*Oliver Wendell Holmes*

Wealth has now all the respect paid to it which is due only to virtue and to talent, but we can see what estimate God places upon it, since he often bestows it upon the meanest and most unworthy of all his creatures.

—*Dean Swift*

Every action of our lives touches on some chord that will vibrate in eternity.

—*E. H. Chapin*

A man's best wealth ought to be himself.

—*William Austin*

THE ARROW AND THE SONG

I shot an arrow into the air,
It fell to earth, I knew not where;
For, so swiftly it flew, the sight
Could not follow it in its flight.

I breathed a song into the air,
It fell to earth, I knew not where;
For who has sight so keen and strong
That it can follow the flight of song?

Long, long afterward, in an oak
I found the arrow, still unbroke;
And the song, from beginning to end,
I found again in the heart of a friend.

—*Henry Wadsworth Longfellow*

I AM MONEY

Dug from the mountainside, washed in the
glen,
Servant am I, or the master of men;
  Steal me, I curse you,
  Earn me, I bless you,
Grasp me and hoard me, a fiend shall pos-
  sess you.
  Lie for me, die for me,
  Covet me, take me.
Angel or devil, I am what you make me.
MONEY.

—*Charles E. Chapler*

PART V
NIGHT

NIGHT

Night. Like a black velvet curtain draped over the noises of the day; like the quietness that comes after a storm; like the coolness to a fevered brow, comes Night.

Man, fulfilled with all he has taken of life from Dawn until Night, serenely folds his robes about him and releases his responsibilities. The Morning Star will shine again, but Man will greet the new day in eternity.

—May Detherage

Now the days are all gone over
Of our singing, love by lover—
Days of summer-colored seas,
Days of many melodies.

Now the nights are all past over
Of our dreaming, where dreams hover
In a mist of fair false things—
Nights with quiet folded wings.

Now the kiss of child and mother,
Now the speech of sister and brother,

Are but with us as strange words,
Or old songs of last year's birds.

Now all good that comes and goes is
As the smell of last year's roses,
As the shining in our eyes
Of dead summer in past skies.

—A. C. Swinburne

SUNSET

The river sleeps beneath the sky,
   And clasps the shadows to its breast;
The crescent moon shines dim on high;
   And in the lately radiant west
   The gold is fading into gray.
   Now stills the lark his festive lay,
   And mourns with me the dying day.

While in the south the first faint star
   Lifts to the night its silver face,
And twinkles to the moon afar
   Across the heaven's graying space,
   Low murmurs reach me from the town,
   As Day puts on her sombre crown,
   And shakes her mantel darkly down.

—Paul Laurence Dunbar

reflection

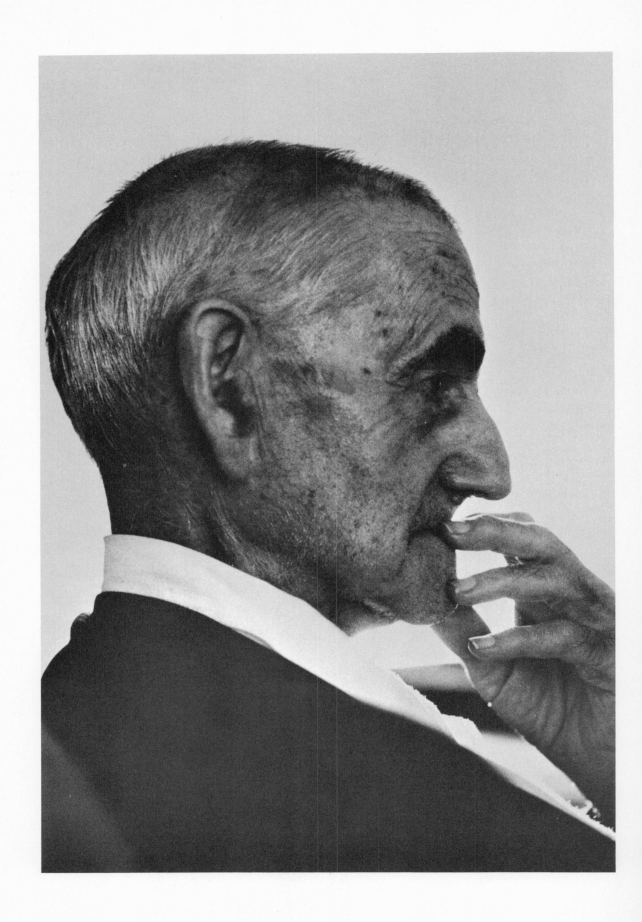

BARTER

Life has loveliness to sell,
   All beautiful and splendid things,
Blue waves whitened on a cliff,
   Soaring fire that sways and sings,
And children's faces looking up
Holding wonder like a cup.

Life has loveliness to sell,
   Music like a curve of gold,
Scent of pine trees in the rain,
   Eyes that love you, arms that hold,
And for your spirit's still delight,
Holy thoughts that star the night.

Spend all you have for loveliness,
   Buy it and never count the cost;
For one white singing hour of peace
   Count many a year of strife well lost,
And for a breath of ecstasy
Give all you have been, or could be.

            —Sara Teasdale

There is a peculiar beauty about godly old age—the beauty of holiness. Husband and wife who have fought the world side by side, who have made common stock of joy or sorrow, and become aged together, are not unfrequently found curiously alike in personal appearance, in pitch and tone of voice, just as twin pebbles on the beach, exposed to the same tidal influences, are each other's alter ego.

            —Alexander Smith

There are two ways of spreading light: to be
The candle or the mirror that reflects it.

            —Edith Wharton

We all seek happiness so eagerly, that in the pursuit we often lose that joyous sense of existence, and those quiet daily pleasures, the values of which our pride alone prevents us from acknowledging.

It has been said with some meaning, that if men would but rest in silence, they might always hear the music of the spheres.

            —Arthur Helps

For age is opportunity no less
Than youth itself, though in another dress,
And as the evening twilight fades away
The sky is filled with stars, invisible by day.

   —Henry Wadsworth Longfellow, from
            "Morituri Salutamus"

SONG TO CELIA

Drink to me only with thine eyes,
   And I will pledge with mine;
Or leave a kiss but in the cup,
   And I'll not look for wine.
The thirst that from the soul doth rise
   Doth ask a drink divine;
But might I of Jove's nectar sup,
   I would not change for thine.

I sent thee late a rosy wreath,
   Not so much honoring thee,
As giving it a hope, that there
   It could not withered be.
But thou thereon didst only breathe,
   And sent'st it back to me;
Since when it grows, and smells, I swear,
   Not of itself, but thee.

            —Ben Jonson

THE DAY IS DONE

The day is done, and the darkness
  Falls from the wings of Night,
As a feather is wafted downward
  From an eagle in his flight.

I see the lights of the village
  Gleam through the rain and the mist,
And a feeling of sadness comes o'er me
  That my soul cannot resist.

A feeling of sadness and longing,
  That is not akin to pain,
And resembles sorrow only,
  As the mist resembles the rain.

Come, read to me some poem,
  Some simple and heartfelt lay,
That shall soothe this restless feeling,
  And banish the thoughts of day.

Not from the grand old masters,
  Not from bards sublime,
Whose distant footsteps echo
  Through the corridors of Time.

For, like strains of martial music,
  Their mighty thoughts suggest
Life's endless toil and endeavor;
  And tonight I long for rest.

Read from some humbled poet,
  Whose songs gushed from his heart,
As showers from the clouds of summer,
  Or tears from eyelids start.

Who, through long days of labor,
  And nights devoid of ease,
Still heard in his soul the music
  Of wonderful melodies.

Such songs have power to quiet
  The restless pulse of care;
And come like the benediction
  That follows after prayer.

Then read from the treasured volume
  The poem of thy choice,
And lend the rhyme of the poet
  The beauty of thy voice.

And the night shall be filled with music,
  And the cares, that infest the day,
Shall fold their tents like the Arabs,
  And as silently steal away.

—*Henry Wadsworth Longfellow*

HOW TO STAY YOUNG

Youth is not a time of life—it is a state of mind.

Nobody grows old by merely living a number of years; people grow old only by deserting their ideals. Years wrinkle the skin, but to give up enthusiasm wrinkles the soul. Worry, doubt, self-distrust, fear and despair—these are the long, long years that bow the head and turn the growing spirit back to dust.

Whether seventy or sixteen, there is in every being's heart the love of wonder, the sweet amazement at the stars and the star-like things and thoughts, the undaunted challenge of events, the unfailing childlike appetite for what next, and the joy and the game of life.

You are as young as your faith, as young as your self-confidence, as old as your fear; as young as your hope, as old as your despair.

—*Samuel Ullman*

The greatest comfort of my old age, and that which gives me the highest satisfaction, is the pleasing remembrance of the many benefits and friendly offices I have done to others.

—*Cato*

IN THE NIGHT

In the night
Grey heavy clouds muffled the valleys,
And the peaks looked toward God alone.
'O Master, that movest the wind with a
    finger,
Humble, idle, futile peaks are we.
Grant that we may run swiftly across the
    world
To huddle in worship at Thy feet.'

In the morning
A noise of men at work came the clear blue
    miles,
And the little black cities were apparent.
'O Master, that knowest the meaning of
    raindrops,
Humble, idle, futile peaks are we.
Give voice to us, we pray, O Lord,
That we may sing Thy goodness to the
    sun.'

In the evening
The far valleys were sprinkled with tiny
    lights.
'O Master,
Thou that knowest the value of kings
    and birds,
Thou hast made us humble, idle, futile
    peaks.
Thou only needst eternal patience;
We bow to Thy wisdom, O Lord—
Humble, idle, futile peaks.'

In the night
Grey heavy clouds muffled the valleys
And the peaks looked toward God alone.

—*Stephen Crane*

Gladstone at eighty had ten times the
weight and power that any man of twenty-
five would have with the same ideals. The
glory of age is only the glory of its enthusiasm, and the respect paid to white hairs
is reverence to a heart fervent, in spite of
the torpid influence of an enfeebled body.
The "Odyssey" was the creation of a blind
old man, but that old man was Homer. . . .

Dandolo, the Doge of Venice, won battles
at ninety-four, and refused a crown at
ninety-six. Wellington planned and super-
intended fortifications at eighty. Bacon
and Humboldt were enthusiastic students
to the last gasp. . . .

Cicero said well that men are like wine:
age sours the bad, and improves the good.

—*O. S. Marden, from*
Pushing to the Front

AUTUMN

Shorter and shorter now the twilight clips
The days, as through the sunset gates they
    crowd.
And Summer from her golden collar slips
And strays through stubble-fields, and
    moans aloud,
Save when by fits the warmer air deceives,
And stealing hopeful to some sheltered
    bower,
She lies on pillows of the yellow leaves,
And tries the old tunes over for an hour.

—*Alice Cury*

MAN-MAKING

We all are blind, until we see
    That in the human plan
Nothing is worth the making if
    It does not make the man.

Why build these cities glorious
    If man unbuilded goes?
In vain we build the work, unless
    The builder also grows.

—*Edwin Markham*

185

TO MY DEAR AND LOVING HUSBAND

If ever two were one, then surely we.
If ever man were lov'd by wife, then thee.
If ever wife was happy in a man,
Compare with me ye women if you can.
I prize thy love more than whole mines of
gold,
Or riches that the East doth hold.
My love is such that Rivers cannot quench,
Nor ought but love from thee, give recom-
pense.
Thy love is such I can no way repay,
The heavens reward thee manifold I pray,
Then while we live, in love let us persevere,
That when we live no more, we may live
ever.

—*Anne Bradstreet*

HURRYING YEARS

For life seems so little when life is past,
And the memories of sorrow flee so fast,
And the woes which were bitter to you and
to me,
Shall vanish as raindrops which fall in the
sea;
And all that has hurt us shall be made good,
And the puzzles which hindered be under-
stood,
And the long, hard march through the
wilderness bare
Seem but a day's journey when once we are
there.

—*Susan Coolidge*

SOMETIMES

Across the fields of yesterday
    He sometimes comes to me,
A little lad just back from play—
    The lad I used to be.

And yet he smiles so wistfully
    Once he has crept within,
I wonder if he hopes to see
    The man I might have been.

—*Thomas S. Jones, Jr.*

THE NEVER-OLD

They who can smile when others hate,
Nor bind the heart with frosts of fate,
Their feet will go with laughter bold
The green roads of the Never-Old.

They who can let the spirit shine
And keep the heart a lighted shrine,
Their feet will glide with fire-of-gold
The green roads of the Never-Old.

They who can put the self aside
And in Love's saddle leap and ride,
Their eyes will see the gates unfold
To green roads of the Never-Old.

—*Edwin Markham*

DAWN

Calmly I rest in this life's evening hour,
Regretful only for so little done
For all human ills, and Him whose kindly
power
Brings me so late to mark life's sinking
sun.

Soon I shall sleep that sleep that knows no
waking,
And quiet rest through all the summer's
bloom,
Waiting the trumpet whose blast, all nature
shaking,
Shall bring a birthday from the opening
tomb.

—*Mark Trafton*

wisdom

OLD LETTERS

I keep your letters for a rainy day;
    Then take them out and read them all
      again.
So, reading, I forget that skies are gray,
    And pathways sodden under falling rain.

They are so full of simple friendliness,—
    Of understanding of the things I love.
No phrase obscure or vague, to make me
      guess,—
    No deep philosophy my soul to move.

And though your eyes are "lifted to the
      hills"
    You still keep faith with earth, and
      earthy things;
Prosaic duty all your hour fills
    The while you listen for the beat of
      wings.

You have read deeply in the book of life,
    And you have added lines that I shall
      keep
To be a shield against the petty strife
    Until such time as I shall fall asleep.

So when I would forget that skies are gray
I read your letters on a rainy day.
              —Adele Jordan Tarr

The wise man guards against the future as
if it were the present.
              —Publilius Syrus

He bids fair to grow wise who has discovered that he is not so.
              —Publilius Syrus

Knowledge and wisdom, far from being
    one,
Have oft times no connection. Knowledge
    dwells
In heads replete with thoughts of other
    men.
Wisdom in minds attentive to their own.
Knowledge is proud that he has learn'd so
    much;
Wisdom is humble that he knows no more.
            —William Cowper, from
                    "The Task"

The mintage of wisdom is to know that rest
is rust, and that real life is in love, laughter
and work.

              —Elbert Hubbard

Life is a progress from want to want, not
from enjoyment to enjoyment.

              —Samuel Johnson

Do not let the good things of life rob you
of the best things.

              —Maltbie D. Babcock

Sincerity and truth are the basis of every
virtue.

              —Confucius

WHEN I KNEW A LITTLE BIT
When I knew a little bit,
Then my silly, blinded wit,
. . . .
Thought it was omniscient; but
When I learned a little more
From the scholar's hoarded store,
Madness' fever soon grew cool,
And I knew I was a fool.

—*Bhartrihari (Sanscrit 651),*
tr. by Arthur W. Ryder

A man shall be commended according to his wisdom: but he that is of a perverse heart shall be despised.

—*Proverbs 12:8*

How few of us keep our minds as well as our eyes open to the things that delight!

—*O. S. Marden, from*
Conquest of Worry

THIS, TOO, WILL PASS
This, too, will pass. O heart, say it over and over,
Out of your deepest sorrow, out of your grief.
No hurt can last forever—perhaps tomorrow
Will bring relief.

This, too, will pass. It will spend itself—its fury
Will die as the wind dies down with the setting sun;

Assuaged and calm, you will rest again, forgetting
A thing that is done.

Repeat it again and again, O heart, for your comfort;
This, too, will pass, as surely as passed before
The old forgotten pain, and the other sorrows
That once you bore.

As certain as stars at night, or dawn after darkness,
Inherent as the lift of the blowing grass,
Whatever your despair or your frustration—
This, too, will pass.

—*Grace Noll Crowell*

For the Lord giveth wisdom: out of his mouth cometh knowledge and understanding. He layeth up sound wisdom for the righteous: he is a buckler to them that walk uprightly. . . .
When wisdom entereth into thine heart, and knowledge is pleasant unto thy soul;
Discretion shall preserve thee, understanding shall keep thee.

—*Proverbs 2:6-7, 10-11*

Conquer a man who never gives by gifts;
Subdue untruthful men by truthfulness;
Vanquish an angry man by gentleness;
And overcome the evil man by goodness.

—*Bhagavad-Gītā*

190

death

IN THE HOSPITAL

Because on the branch that is tapping my
    pane
  A sun-wakened leaf-bud, uncurled,
Is bursting its rusty brown sheathing in
    twain,
  I know there is Spring in the world.

Because through the sky-patch whose azure
    and white
  My window frames all the day long
A yellowbird dips in a billow of flight,
  I know there is Song.

Because even here in this Mansion of Woe
  Where creep the dull hours, leaden-shod,
Compassion and Tenderness aid me, I know
  There is God.

              —*Arthur Guiterman*

The young may die, but the old must.

      —*Henry Wadsworth Longfellow, from*
          "The Golden Legend"

The man who has caught a glimpse of his
divine possibilities, who is conscious of the
Changeless, divine Presence, has the courage to face whatever comes to him without
a doubt or tremor. He knows that being a
part of the Life, of the Great Cause, he is
secure from all harm. Such a man has no
fear of the change called death, and of the
body's dissolution, because he knows that
he is a part of deathless life, of indestructi-
bility.

          —*O. S. Marden, from*
          Conquest of Worry

Death is the chillness that precedes the
    dawn;
We shudder for a moment, then awake
In the broad sunshine of the other life.

    —*Henry Wadsworth Longfellow, from*
           "Michael Angelo"

WHEN SHE MUST GO

When she must go, so much will go with
    her!
  Stories of country summers, far and
    bright,
Wisdom of berries, flowers and chestnut
    bur,
  And songs to comfort babies in the night;

Old legends and their meanings, half-lost
    tunes,
  Wise craftsmanship in all the household
    ways,
And roses taught to flower in summer
    noons,
  And children taught the shaping of good
    days;

A heart still steadfast, stable, that can know
  A son's first loss, a daughter's first heart-
    break,
And say to them, "This, too, shall pass and
    go;
  This is not all!" while anguished for
    their sake;

Courage to cling to when the day is lost,
  Love to come back to when all love grows
    cold,
Quiet from tumult; hearth fire from the
    frost.
  Oh, must she ever go, and we be old?

          —*Margaret Widdemer*

LIFE

Alas for him who never sees
The stars shine through his cypress-trees!
Who, hopeless, lays his dead away,
Nor looks to see the breaking day
Across the mournful marbles play!
Who hath not learned, in hours of faith,
The truth to flesh and sense unknown,
That Life is ever Lord of Death,
And Love can never lose its own!

—*John Greenleaf Whittier*

WHEN NIGHT IS ALMOST DONE

When Night is almost done—
And Sunrise grows so near
That we can touch the Spaces,
It's time to smooth the Hair—

And get the Dimples ready—
And wonder we could care
For that old-faded Midnight—
That frightened—but an Hour—

—*Emily Dickinson*

UNTIL THE SHADOWS LENGTHEN

O Lord, support us all the day long of this
    troublesome life,
Until the shadows lengthen,
And the evening comes,
And the busy world is hushed,
And the fever of life is over,
And our work is done.
Then of the mercy
Grant us a safe lodging,
And a holy rest,
And peace at the last:
Through Jesus Christ our Lord. Amen.

—*John Henry Newman*

Come, lovely and soothing death,
Undulate round the world, serenely arriv-
    ing, arriving,
In the day, in the night, to all, to each,
Sooner or later delicate death.

Praised be the fathomless universe,
For life and joy, and for objects and knowl-
    edge curious,
For love, sweet love—but praise! praise!
    praise!
For the sure-enwinding arms of cool-en-
    folding death.

.   .   .   .

The night in silence under many a star,
The ocean shore and the husky whispering
    wave whose voice I know,
And the soul turning to thee, O vast and
    well-veiled death,
And the body gratefully nestling close to
    thee.

—*Walt Whitman, from
"When Lilacs Last in the
Dooryard Bloomed"*

MY LIFE CLOSED TWICE

My life closed twice before its close;
It yet remains to see
If Immortality unveil
A third event to me,

So huge, so hopeless to conceive
As these that twice befel.
Parting is all we know of heaven,
And all we need of hell.

—*Emily Dickinson*

DEATH IS A DOOR

Death is only an old door
  Set in a garden wall.
On quiet hinges it gives at dusk,
  When the thrushes call.

Along the lintel are green leaves,
  Beyond, the light lies still;
Very weary and willing feet
  Go over that sill.

There is nothing to trouble any heart,
  Nothing to hurt at all.
Death is only an old door
  In a garden wall.

              —Nancy Byrd Turner

DEATH, BE NOT PROUD

Death, be not proud, though some have
  called thee
Mighty and dreadful, for thou art not so;
For those whom thou think'st thou dost
  overthrow
Die not, poor Death; nor yet canst thou
  kill me.
From Rest and Sleep, which but thy Pic-
  ture be,
Much pleasure; then from thee much more
  must flow;
And soonest our best men with thee do
  go—
Rest of their bones and souls' delivery!
Thou'rt slave to fate, chance, kinds, and
  desperate men,
And dost with poison, war, and sickness
  dwell;
And poppy or charms can make us sleep
  as well
And better than thy stroke. Why swell'st
  thou then?
  One short sleep past, we wake eternally,
  And Death shall be no more: Death, thou
    shalt die!

              —John Donne

At last we will all have to start on that
dark, perilous journey. We must all die,
and go out beyond the air and up through
the stars.

              —A. A. Hodges

Christ is risen! There is life, therefore, after
death! His resurrection is the symbol and
pledge of universal resurrection!

              —Lyman Beecher

A LITTLE WHILE

It is so natural that we fall asleep
  Like tired children when the day is done,
That I would question why the living weep
  When Death has kissed the laughing lips
    of one.
We do not sigh when golden skies have
  donned
  The purple shadows and the gray of
    night,
Because we know the morning lies beyond,
  And we must wait a little while for light.

So when, grown weary with the care and
  strife
  Our loved ones find in sleep, the peace
    they crave,
We should not weep, but learn to count
  this life
  A prelude to the one beyond the grave;
And thus be happy for them, not distressed,
  But lift our hearts with love to God and
    smile,
And we, anon, like tired ones will rest
  If we will hope and wait—a little while.

              —Ella Bentley

AT LAST

When on my day of life the night is falling,
　　And, in the winds from unsunned spaces
　　　　blown,
I hear far voices out of darkness calling
　　My feet to paths unknown.

Thou who hast made my home of life so
　　　　pleasant,
　　Leave not its tenant when its walls
　　　　decay;
O Love Divine, O Helper ever present,
　　Be Thou my strength and stay!

Be near me when all else is from me drift-
　　　　ing:
　　Earth, sky, home's pictures, days of shade
　　　　and shine,
And kindly faces to my own uplifting
　　The love which answers mine.

I have but Thee, my Father! let Thy Spirit
　　Be with me then to comfort and uphold;
No gate of pearl, no branch of palm I
　　　　merit,
　　Nor street of shining gold.

Suffice it if—my good and ill unreckoned,
　　And both forgiven through Thy abound-
　　　　ing grace—
I find myself by hands familiar beckoned
　　Unto my fitting place.

Some humble door among Thy many man-
　　　　sions,
　　Some sheltering shade where sin and
　　　　striving cease,
And flows for ever through heaven's green
　　　　expansions
　　The river of Thy peace.

There, from the music round about me
　　　　stealing,
　　I fain would learn the new and holy
　　　　song,

And find at last, beneath Thy trees of heal-
　　　　ing,
　　The life for which I long.

—*John Greenleaf Whittier*

THE CHARIOT

Because I could not stop for Death—
He kindly stopped for me—
The Carriage held but just Ourselves—
And Immortality.

We slowly drove—He knew no haste
And I had put away
My labor and my leisure too,
For His Civility—

We passed the School, where Children
　　　　strove,
At Recess—in the Ring—
We passed the Fields of Gazing Grain—
We passed the Setting Sun—

Or rather—He passed Us—
The Dews drew quivering and chill—
For only Gossamer, my Gown—
My Tippet—only Tulle—

We paused before a House that seemed
A Swelling of the Ground—
The Roof was scarcely visible—
The Cornice—in the Ground—

Since then—'tis Centuries—and yet
Feels shorter than the Day
I first surmised the Horses Heads
Were toward Eternity—

—*Emily Dickinson*

196

THINGS THAT NEVER DIE

The pure, the bright, the beautiful
　　That stirred our hearts in youth,
The impulses to wordless prayer,
　　The streams of love and truth,
The longing after something lost,
　　The spirit's yearning cry,
The striving after better hopes—
　　These things can never die.

The timid hand stretched forth to aid
　　A brother in his need;
A kindly word in grief's dark hour
　　That proves a friend indeed;
The plea for mercy softly breathed,
　　When justice threatens high,
The sorrow of a contrite heart—
　　These things shall never die.

Let nothing pass, for every hand
　　Must find some work to do,
Lose not a chance to waken love—
　　Be firm and just and true.
So shall a light that cannot fade
　　Beam on thee from on high,
And angel voices say to thee—
　　"These things shall never die."

　　　　　　　　—Charles Dickens

SUNDOWN

When my sun of life is low,
　　When the dewy shadows creep,
Say for me before I go
　　"Now I lay me down to sleep."

I am at the journey's end,
　　I have sown and I must reap;
There are no more ways to mend—
　　Now I lay me down to sleep.

Nothing more to doubt or dare,
　　Nothing more to give or keep;
Say for me the children's prayer,
　　"Now I lay me down to sleep."

Who has learned along the way—
　　Primrose path or stony steep—
More of wisdom than to say,
　　"Now I lay me down to sleep"?

What have you more wise to tell
　　When shadows round me creep?
All is over, all is well—
　　Now I lay me down to sleep.

　　　　　　　　—Bert Leston Taylor

He that heareth my word, and believeth on him that sent me, hath everlasting life, and shall not come into condemnation; but is passed from death unto life.

　　　　　　　　—John 5:24

Under the wide and starry sky,
Dig the grave and let me lie.
Glad did I live and gladly die,
　　And I laid me down with a will.

This be the verse you grave for me:
"Here he lies where he longed to be;
Home is the sailor, home from sea,
　　And the hunter home from the hill."

　　　　　　—Robert Louis Stevenson,
　　　　　　　　　　　"Requiem"

Death is delightful. Death is dawn,
The waking from a weary night
Of fever unto truth and light.

　　　—Joaquin Miller, from "Even So"

INDEXES

INDEX OF TITLES AND FIRST LINES

INDEX OF SUBJECTS